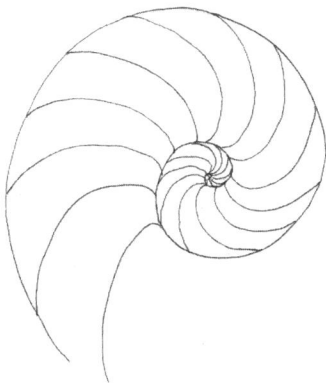

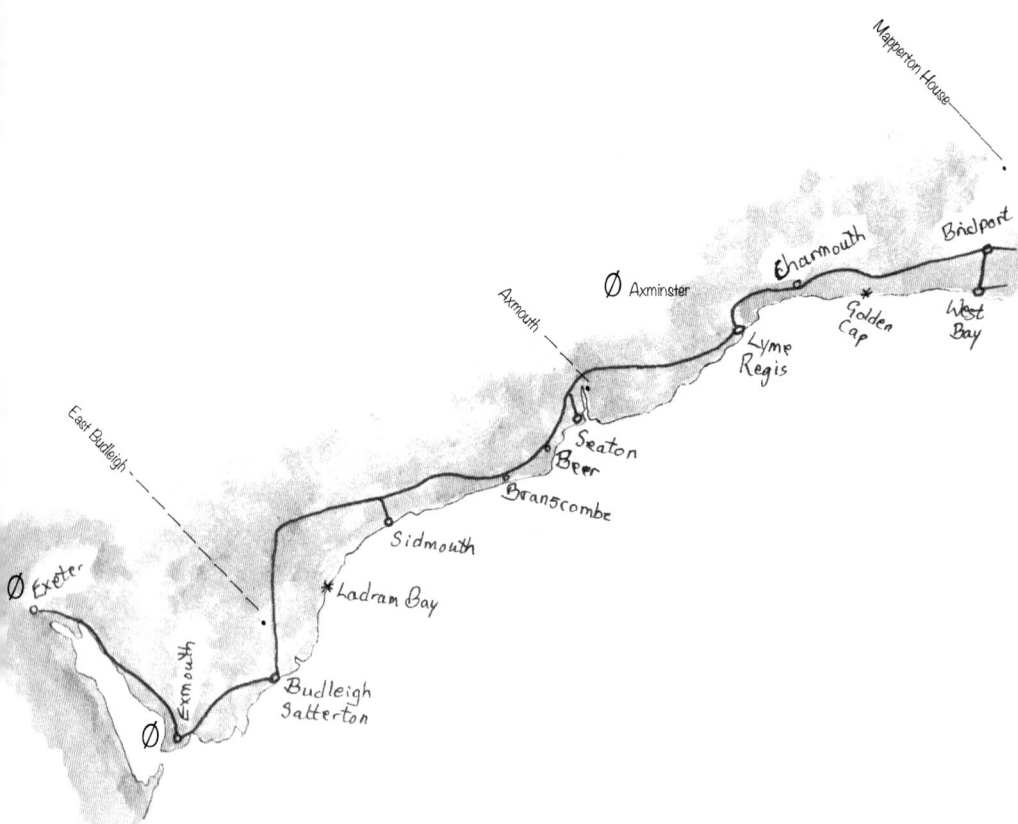

Brownsea

Ø Poole

Bournemouth

Ø Wareham

Studland

Ø Wool

Norden ° Corfe

Swanage

Ø Dorchester

Osmington

Kimmeridge

Burton Bradstock

Lulworth

Langton Matravers

Worth Matravers

Abbotsbury

St Aldhan's Head

Ø Weymouth

* Portland Bill

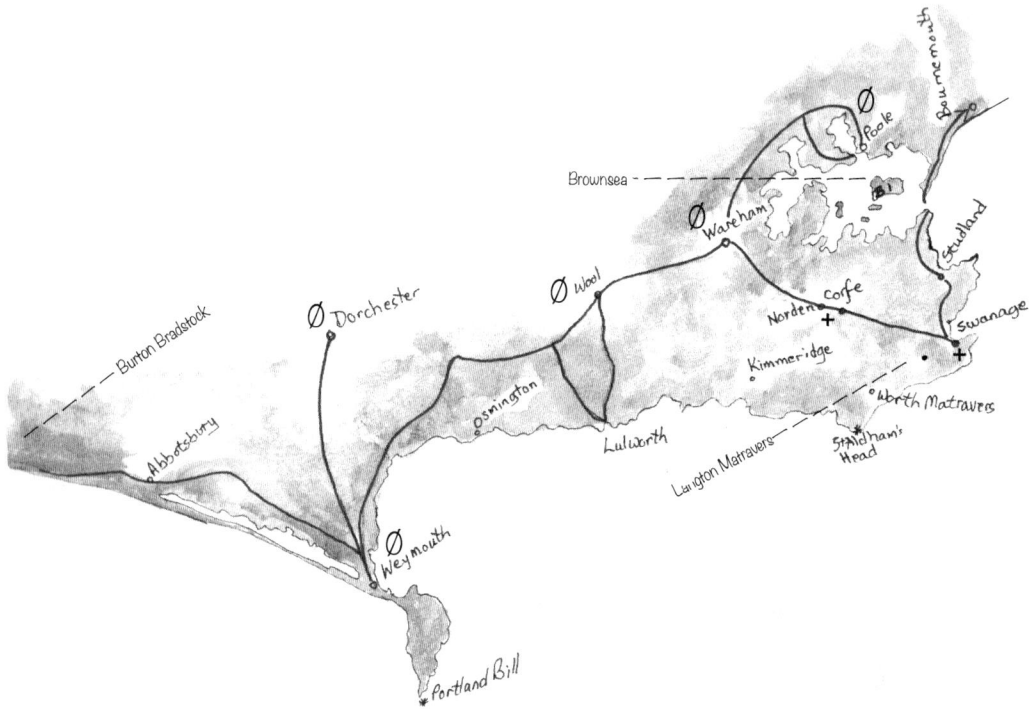

the jurassic coast

—— buses all year

Ø   train stations

+   steam train

N

the wonder coast

skipping along a coastal delight

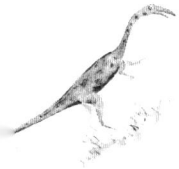

iain dryden

author & artist

Studland to Exmouth

a tread westwards through time
or
a journey to dip in and out of

disclaimer

this book is neither guide nor geological study
for I am no expert,
the spirit is awe

unconventionally,
each double-page layout
has been treated uniquely

contents

any walk without reverence is a sad walk,
a walk which induces wonder is a grand walk indeed

a wee start

A word of caution, a delightful revolution could happen as you begin this enchanting journey heading westwards back through time, back through space. History both recent and vast is in the landscape, in the hedgerows, it is in the rocks and weathered farmsteads, it lingers in local legends. This stunning landscape, this World Heritage Site where one third of life on Earth is revealed, has dinosaurs lurking in the cliffs and fossils hiding upon the beaches. And between the many outstanding natural wonders there are pockets of hope, projects attempting to revive our fertile planet.

These pages, a potpourri of information, take you along each curve of this exciting coastline, they let you linger in artful corners and be drawn into charmed settlements. Each rise provides a moment to be still. Facing the enormity of time, our boggling origins, our part in the vast scheme of things... we sense our mortality, our power, our own significance. Such respect encourages responsibility, a wish to cherish our surroundings, to act as best we can to save this fragile gem suspended in the icy cold of space.

Had he sculpted this strip of South Western England, Slatibartfast, the Coastal Designer Supreme* who preferred happiness to truth, would have been content.

*Hitchhiker's Guide to the Galaxy

Studland Bay

studland bay

Riding the River Frome's outflow from the glittering expanse of
Poole Harbour, huge cargo ships and small sailing boats slip
past the car ferry bobbing over to Studland Bay. The banks
guarding this narrow exit could hardly be different. Sandbanks,
where every inch costs a fortune, is the city's last gasp, whilst the
expanse of Studland has altered little in a thousand years.
Curiously, both shores are growing, Sandbanks' quartzite grains
drift along from the beaches of Bournemouth whereas
Studland's chalky sands come from the pristine white cliffs
ahead.

Such constant nibbling illustrates the fleeting reality of the
Earth's landscapes and of life itself, which has often been pushed
to the edge. The intricate web of life is fragile, yet its very basis
has inbuilt resilience, as the walk ahead which oscillates between
humanity's presence and the Earth's past, illustrates.

Sipping champagne upon their terraces, Sandbanks' modern day merchant princes gaze out at Brownsea Island, the largest of the green blobs floating upon the lagoon's broad, surface. Guarding this ecological gem is one of King Henry VIII's ornate castles. Ostensibly erected in 1545 to protect Poole from the French whose modern liner/ferries glide past daily, it could well have been a seaside indulgence for the luxury loving king.

On Brownsea Island, offering youngsters guidance on character building through the medium of respecting the great outdoors, Baden-Powell hosted the first Scout camp in 1907. Fittingly, within this haven, the National Trust and the Dorset Wildlife Trust protect the rare red squirrel.

It is hard to imagine that Poole's spacious lagoon was once a green valley through which the River Frome gurgled. Here outside the harbour beyond Sandbanks, try to mentally encompass this inland sea with an unbroken ridge reaching from the white cliffs ahead to the distant Isle of Wright. Such a bulk of land once sheltered the Frome as it flowed off to join the Solent and stream around the Isle of Wight, to merge with a 'Euro' torrent gushing from Rotterdam as well as Le Havre.

Peering across this bay you might assume that the arrival of the first Brits was a water-walking miracle. Sadly not. As with all supernatural tales, their story is more mundane. Skirting to the north of that Euro deluge, hunter-gatherers chased deer and soft coated ponies to southern England; some eventually arrived here. Those ancient genus horses still roam the nearby New Forest, though semi-wild today, they are privately owned, some perhaps by the descendants of those first settlers.

part of Poole harbour, sketched from Studland's heathlands

This benign scene where your feet tread soft sands, where sunbathers and swimmers enjoy the balmy waters, was once semi-arctic tundra. As the ice coating Europe began melting 10-12,000 years ago sea levels rose to swamp the Euro river and fill the English Channel. Five thousand years of wild storms broke the chalk ridge, severing the Isle of Wight from Purbeck, flooding this low green interior, creating the Portsmouth-Solent-Poole complex of harbours, drowning the Frome in salty water up to Wareham's lively edge.

As the climate warmed, Aegean farmers steadily moved north from the eastern Mediterranean, some drifted up the Rhone, absorbing resident hunter-gatherers. A few hardy types discovered Britain* and their expanding population inhabited Studland's sandy hills, today their burial mounds decorate Godlingston Heath. These agriculturalists actively changed the environment. To feed their recently domesticated animals they cut back the oak and ash forest. Imagine the feisty Middle Eastern woman who first tamed the long horned auroch, 1.80 metres at the shoulder. Those super-cows, ancestor of all cows, include the South Devons which the National Trust has brought here to help retain the area's open character.

* dates aren't given as research is contradictory

Pathways lure the respectful to explore a frangible complexity of ecosystems so special that much of it is a classified Site of Specific Scientific Interest. There are mudflats where long legged migrating birds feast, salt marshes filled with a myriad of mysterious creatures, dunes wriggling with reptiles and hills bursting with unusual plants. Tread carefully so as not to harm the sneaky slow worm, scare the scarce sand lizard or alarm the languid adder, to say nothing of nailing a hard to be seen newt. Here lies Britain's richest area of wild flora, it sustains bountiful bees, flitting butterflies and multiple rare moths.

Should you spot dragonflies, do a skip! They have survived tremendous upheavals and remain intact in a design pre-dating dinosaurs. As are parts of you. You, a mere link at the end of a long, involved mega-story reaching far back beyond the Jurassic, have an inner ear refined in Triassic reptiles. Your mammalian ear flaps have the added advantage of collecting sound waves, and you have a refined ear-drum to translate airwaves into your favourite music. Tune in with attention, as did early mammals to jump from being juiced by dinosaur jaws, and absorb the waves caressing this curve of sand.

The bay's serene waters are famed as the UK's only place where both the spiny and the short-snouted seahorses exist together. Not that long ago, they were virtually unable to breed in what had once been their ideal nursery, so in 2019 Studland Bay was made a protected Marine Conservation Zone. Lockdown in 2020 speeded up their recovery. Fewer private boats allowed the rare seagrass to regenerate, encouraging 46 individual seahorses, as well as rays and other uncommon creatures, to return. Lockdown ended. They fled. Today a new voluntary no-anchoring zone is being tested with the hopeful cooperation of boat owners. Pray that it works, for sea grass meadows are dense biodiverse habitats hosting hundreds of species; the plants are also high absorbers of CO_2, locking this destructive gas in their roots.

Thanks to insightful conservationists, pockets of nature are cared for all along the 90 odd miles of this path that steps over a huge chunk of life's turbulent history. You've now met two, the Dorset Wildlife Trust and the National Trust, manned mainly by volunteers. The National Trust nurtures the entirety of Studland so spending your pounds in their shops, cafes and car parks protects this treasure. The Studland estate was bequeathed to the Trust in 1981 by the Bankes family, who also donated nearby Corfe Castle and the Kingston Lacey estate. The Trust have leased the Bankes' seaside retreat to a lush hotel chain. Also leased out is Harry Warren House, an old hunting lodge whose gates you'll pass on the way to see Old Harry; and various cottages are in private hands with planning controls ensuring Studland village retains its classic Dorset character.

The area's sublime peace was disrupted during World War II when Allied troops trained for the liberation of northern France. Solid proof of this dire period is found in the well hidden concrete lump of Harry's Fort, from within which Churchill, Eisenhower and several generals watched their forces undertake exercises which would prove vital to the success of D-Day. During the complicated night before D-Day, not far away upon the dreamy cliffs of the Isle of Wight, Britain's secret Radar unit played a vital role.

My mother was in charge of the chart-table plotting that audacious undertaking. Leaving the bunker at dawn for a break, she gasped at what she saw. "It was astounding. The air was a ceiling of aircraft, the Solent was carpeted with ships. Until that moment, involved in my own specific duties, I was largely unaware of what our brave little country was preparing with our Allies."

Studland was long known as marginal; one wonders if, in the centuries before D-Day, the aristocratic Bankes family knew how many smugglers used their semi-wild terrain to land and disseminate contraband. The gangs hid it in the sand dunes, in the dead of night they rowed it across Poole harbour's weave of inlets and islands. Impossible to follow them through the swampy terrain astride the River Frome which they knew better than the government troops tracking them.

Protected by Old Harry, pirates such as Harry Paye waited for merchant ships. Raising the skull and cross bones to the tops of their masts they rushed out to capture French, Dutch and Spanish craft. Smuggling, though risky, was a rewarding activity for there were many keen customers. The harsh economics imposed on the poor, enticed entire families, indeed whole villages to be involved in contraband. It is said that women and children often pelted government officers with pebbles.

Choose a comfortable pebble from the golden sand and let your mind wander back 2.6 million years to when humanity invented the knife. Apes wield stones to break nuts and defend themselves but we fashioned useful implements from obsidian, flint and other rocks that cleave with sharp edges. Tools improved our existence, they helped grow our brains. No wonder pebbles and stone circles are still so appealing. Stroking your time smoothed pebble, move towards those intoxicating white cliffs ahead. Slow down, allow the lulling waves to rise from the depths of nowhere to massage your mind, ease your wandering mood.

a local flint in a grump

Old Harry guarding Studland Bay

old harry & co

Having traversed the timeless greenery adorning Studland village, the path rises to the headland. Where it levels, a large boulder has within it the enticing shape of old roots. Thought to be from the petrified forest which covered Poole Harbour about 45 millions years ago, there's more down on Redend Point, but they are not. They're actually the clumping growth of inorganic pyrites crystals.

This little rise bathed in birdsong is a geological fault created by an earthquake which lifted the block you have arrived upon. It is quite a dramatic moment. You have left the present era and are now stood upon chalk strata laid down during the preceding period, the Cretaceous.

This step arguably* marks the final moment the dinosaurs existed 66 million years ago. Ending the Cretaceous period, a huge meteor created a crater 20 miles deep by 120 miles wide in the Gulf of Mexico. Vaporised rock and sulphur filled the atmosphere, burning the ground, bringing 10 sunless years; 75% of all species globally died. This was the final act of the Cretaceous Extinction*. Of the dinosaurs, who had evolved to fill every environmental niche and had been around for an astonishing 160 million years, only the ancestors of our birds survived. Scavenger species living off detritus also lived on - mammals suddenly had space to thrive.

66 million years ago

* See P190

We *Homo sapiens* who have yet to survive half a million years owe our existence to the Cretaceous Extinction. Sadly, local evidence of the worldwide scatter of iridium dust from that gigantic impact has thus far not been detected along this fault line, unless you dear reader are undertaking groundbreaking research. The Cretaceous was the last of four major mass extinctions our planet has witnessed. Today during the Anthropocene (human) era, more than 16% of species in Britain (& 28% world-wide) are threatened with extinction due to habitat loss and other existential threats.

On a sunny summer's weekend the walk atop the chalk cliffs to Old Harry is popular, yet worth it. Whilst light played over the sparkling expanse of water to my left, as voices from around the world drifted about me, I bent down to observe bees boring into the hard-trodden track. Their little legs kicked out soil creating small damp mounds upon the baked surface. "Why here to be flattened by so many shoes?" asked a Japanese woman.

Inside a multi-stemmed mine, the miner bee lays her eggs, each sealed off from the others. When she finally closes the shaft, utterly alone, the larvae will hatch to feast on pollen she has left. When satiated they spin cocoons within which the lazy youngsters hibernate all summer and winter, miraculously emerging from the ground in spring as adult bees. They don't live long. Airborne males have only two weeks to mate before dying, and she, once impregnated, has just six frantic flying weeks to dig, lay and gather infant food, before her own life terminates.

Such a high risk, short term strategy obviously works, for insects were around 541 million years ago, way before dinos stomped about. There was once enough oxygen for superbugs to thrive - imagine dragonflies with 0.75 metre wingspans and millipedes 2.5 metre long. The wonder of nature.

A couple of wee tracks to your left cut through the low trees, follow one and you'll discover a patch of magic suspended above the glowing white cliffs. The view out over the bay towards the urban glint of Poole and Bournemouth is arresting. There is something special about the sheer whiteness of the cliffs around Handfast Point. Tiny ivory peninsulas, each so perfectly artistic, rise from the clear sea. Yet beware of that drop, chalk crumbles.

The inner cringe, that fear of heights, is no more than our alerted body saying, 'Step back'. Misunderstanding the workings of the brain, we assume the mind has flipped. Not at all. The brain prepares us for danger and the body believes the brain's intense conjurings - a rope becoming a snake is better than being bitten. To escape being eaten, we are programmed to be alert, anxious, forgetting this, we tie ourselves in mental knots, but we can play on this when next hit by a wave of anxiety (or discomfort).

Escaping this trap takes a bit of commitment yet it is well worth it and is so simple and so soothing. As you enjoy a few relaxing breaths, know you are generally safe where you are; delight in being alive; feel lucky to be human! Our beings are truly extraordinary. Visualise yourself as a bright, balanced being firmly implanted. Fake it till it becomes true, researchers have found this happens (for those conjuring reasons).

Old Harry & pals

Some say the devil fell asleep on this headland, hence the name Old Harry's Rocks. Probable? Others claim Harry was a Viking called Earl Harold who drowned here and became a pillar of rock. Obviously. Then there's that pirate Harry Paye. Maybe. Certainly the devil was in all three.

A quadruple whammy crumbled Old Harry, his wife and pals. Rainwater being slightly acidic wears away the calcium in the chalk. The second degrader - powerful storm waves plaster the cliffs in salt which seeps in to eat the structure. Thirdly, drying salt swells to opens up minute fissures. Lastly, soil upon cliff tops without much vegetational cover expands with rain and increases erosion.

Along the stretch facing out to sea there's a series of baby coves intricately sculptured by southwestern storms. Off-white cliffs with thin layers of subtly darker stone, neat beaches, quite a treat to behold. Fissures widen into cracks, these enlarge, cut back, thinned by waves, thin spars of land emerge. Larger cracks become caves, which eventually bite through the spars, forming arches. These finally collapse, leaving stacks which stand alone - hey presto! dear old Harry, his wife and friends gossip on a solid platform as their feet are caressed by waves.

Upon this narrowing jut of land where the sea expands towards the distant horizon, stands creation's best bit of kit. You! A marvel to treasure each hour. What a spirit in which to tread this terrain filled with riches.

météo fenêtre

(window forecast)

England is an Atlantic island and rain gear should always be to hand. Weather apps can put you in trouble, so why not become a mini weather watcher:

Low heavy cloud stuck together (strato-cumulus) = easily six hours 'as-is-now' conditions.

Fluffy sheep (cumulus) = fair weather. Seen mid-morning, dry weather till sunset.

Giant and billowing (cumulo-nimbus) = can bring scattered summer storms.

Feathery cloud strips (cirrus) = a depression is 15-24 hours away. If they have thickly set lines, expect heavy inclemency.

Small dark tatty ghosts hanging beneath clouds or cloud banks = imminent rain very likely.

But don't quote me, British weather is capricious!

the chalk ridge rushing westwards, sketched from Norden

the chalk ridge

Arching towards the sky, grass upon chalk. Brainwashed by fresh sea air, you rise up this coastal ridge with its superb overview of the impressive landscape. See again how this bulk of chalk once ran east to the Isle of Wight. The strata, vaguely horizontal at Old Harry, now slopes down to the north, dipping beneath Studland and Poole harbour to rise again in those distant hills. This chalk also tilts upwards as you move towards Ballard Down and the southern slope plunges into Swanage Bay. Such are the contortions of our continents bumping into one another.

If you were to have been here roughly 95 million years ago, you would be swimming through a warm tropical sea covering much of modern England and France. These colossal spans of time are hard for recently formed creatures such as us to sense, but trying makes it easier.

95 mya

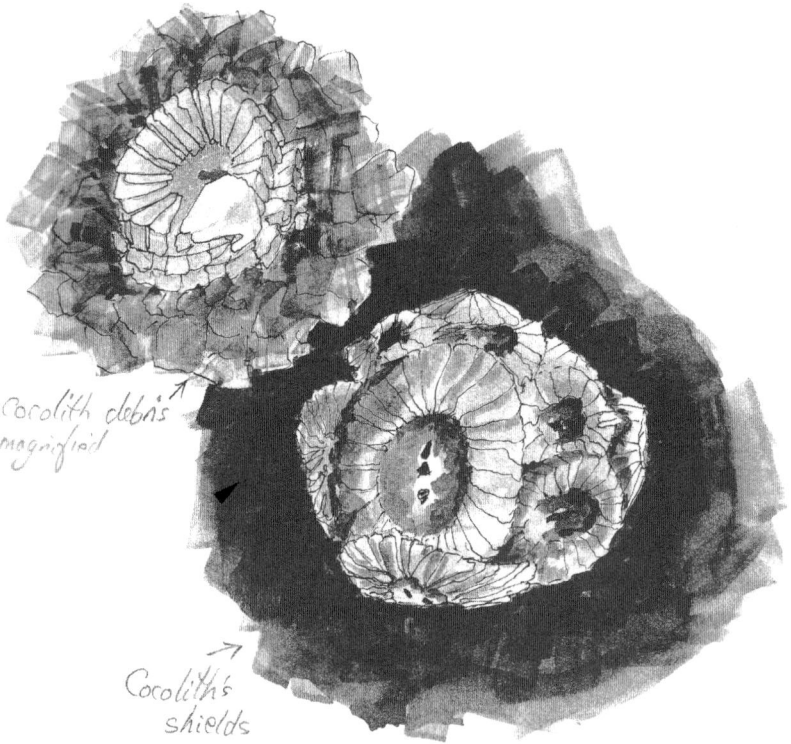

Cocolith debris
magnified

Cocolith's
shields

For the next 30 million years you'd have seen trillions of zillions of calcite snowflakes - minute calcium disc-shields discarded by a group of algae called the *coccolith*. Falling and settling on the sea bed, one on top of the other, they solidified into the chalk strata which continues a few hundred metres beneath the soles of your feet. This chalk spreads north beyond those rolling hills over the far side of Poole harbour, it is found in Normandy, champagne is grown upon it and it is found in other places. That is a staggering amount of creatures constantly discarding their protective pinhead sized shields.

These weeny wee algae still exist and they are the most calcium productive items on earth. This great carbon sink maybe one of our saviours. Being part of the plankton plethora, they are the main base of the complex oceanic food chain, so everything from whales to snails depends on their bloom. Relatives of *coccoliths* are also responsible for 50% of the air we breathe, having many million of years ago added oxygen to the Earth's once poisonous atmosphere. Take a welcoming breath and sigh a thousand thanks to these extraordinary little things.

From up here on Ballard Down you can see right over the eastern part of the Isle of Purbeck. Can you see that this running ridge of chalk defines and divides Purbeck, holding back the swampy Frome lands to the north? If you were to ignite your jet pack and fly high, you'd find it to be broken by Corfe Gap. The more environmentally conscious might tramp across Swanage's fertile valley of sands and clays, heading towards the fine views upon the distant limestone ridge which abuts the sea.

Corfe Gap - a break in the chalk ridge with Poole harbour
and the continuing chalk uplands beyond

corfe

Bronze Age barrows show that people were living on Corfe Common 6,000 years ago. Swish forwards to the year 875 when the Saxon King Alfred built a classic wooden castle on Corfe Gap, a perfect mound set within a narrow slit in this chalk ridge. Alfred undertook his building spree after repelling a Viking invasion off Swanage, where he sank 120 ships, with the aid of a storm - dear Old Harry was on his side. One hundred years later Corfe Castle witnessed Queen Aelfrida murder her stepson, King Edward and install her son Ethelred the Unready, which triggered many more years of Viking attacks, because, well, he was unready in too many ways.

Then came the 1066 invasion by more Norsemen, namely the Franco-Vikings, who replaced Saxon lords with Norman ones. Old Harry, where were your storms? To be fair, they had thwarted earlier Norman efforts. Old Harry was definitely asleep when the Saxon troops trekked all the way across England, having defeated another load of Vikings (who were helped by Harold's own deceitful brother Tostig). Battle weary, they marched from Stamford Bridge in Yorkshire and, at Battle in Sussex, they lost to William the Viko-Norman.

Boasting their power, the Normans artfully rebuilt Corfe Castle as one of a few English stone constructions since Roman times. They stole chunks of land from the Saxons, who had swiped it from the Celts who've left their genes in 64% of the British. The Celt warriors had previously nudged aside the Britons, who had earlier sent the hunter-gathers galloping, even though their feisty great grannies had trotted over here with grazing ponies. How wonderful, our England is a mongrel nation.

Indicating Portland's importance, some 120 years after the Normans arrived, King John expanded Corfe Castle with an outer curtain wall, a plush hall and a fine chapel. He stored some of his royal treasures here as well as impounding his French niece Eleanor, whose brother he had killed earlier for contesting the English throne; 22 of her noble French knights starved to death in Corfe's dank dungeon. The year before his death, in 1215, John's Norman barons, polluted by living amongst us Saxon/Celt/Picts, forced John to abandon absolutist French autocratic rule by accepting the civil liberties inscribed in the Magna Carta. Two years later they had to force his reluctant son Henry III to do the same, laying the roots of our British Constitution....

Rolling onwards roughly 400 years and Corfe Castle passed into the private hands of Sir Christopher Hatton, Queen Elizabeth's Lord Chancellor and Admiral of the Purbeck Fleet. This allowed Sir C. to capture, ie pirate, foreign ships (at this time Europe was a collective of rascal fiefdoms). Corfe Castle was bought in 1635 by Sir John Bankes, Lord Chief Justice of England and attorney-general to King Charles I, with whom he sided during the Civil War. His abandoned wife, 'Brave Dame Mary', valiantly defended the prestigious castle against Cromwell's anti-royalists. Eventually betrayed by one of her own officers, the Parliamentarians snuck in to the castle and she was captured. In a fit of jealousy a couple of years later, those rabid fanatics blew the majestic place to bits. The iconic remains haunt many a film and book, and add charm to the quaint old settlement nestled at its feet.

One of the more enticing sounds of civilisation, a tooting steam train, enlivens the area as it trundles back and forth between Norden and Swanage. Swanage Railway Line claims to contribute millions to the local economy as well as taking roughly 40,000 cars off the winding roads due to its Park & Ride scheme. This roughly balances CO_2 emissions but it certainly diminishes pollutants and eases the lanes. The railway came into being to move quality Purbeck stone and clay to market. At Norden, there's an inspiring clay museum which asks only for a donation.

Corfe's beguiling ancient settlement is surrounded by Corfe Common, where local families grazed (and over-grazed) livestock and harvested wood. The common is a lucky survivor. Between 1604 and 1914 over 5,200 Enclosure Bills were enacted across this little country, removing 20% of Britain's agricultural land from public use, arguably forcing many to find work in towns. Serious riots erupted across the land in 1549 and 1607. No wonder whole villages began smuggling.

During the English revolution of 1642, Cromwell lured the public by speaking against large landlords stealing common land. Once his revolution succeeded and 'his people' took this to heart, Cromwell sided with the rich and moved against the popular Leveller and Digger movements.

Enclosures undoubtably improved productivity, but the land gave fewer people an income. Enclosure also changed the landscape, generating more of the hedges and fences which add to Britain's charm. Since a valuable ancient coin stash was found on Corfe Common, the National Trust banned metal detectors, so beware if you'd planned to use yours.

"Provide open-air sitting rooms for the poor," Octavia Hill said in 1895 when she and others formed the National Trust. They were inspired by John Ruskin, as well as by American pro-nature movements who argued for the right of the people to walk through nature. In the early 1900's the Trust started to save stately homes from ruin as the owners couldn't afford to keep them up. Today this far-sighted charity owns over 200 historic houses, 41 castles and more than 1,300 tenant farms, as well as protecting swathes of unspoiled countryside and coastline through which the public can roam with loaded cameras.

Enhance your walk by casting yourself as a master of photography. Ambling through this attractive village, focus your lens on an unusual door, a colourful leaf, a bright insect, what ever captures your fancy. True art arises from moments when the attention is childlike, unbiased, open to what is.

Art is just one joyful skip from our usual mindsets.

Mindsets, people assume, are cast in iron, but unquestioned attitudes inherited from our families, subcultures and societies are malleable. Equally sane people in different circumstances can have opposite mindsets. That is one of the joys of travel, you discover the world abounds with a multitude of stances and values. Ergo, you can change yours without falling apart.

haunting Corfe

swanage bay

Reaching back from the sea, behind Swanage's urban containment, lies a patchwork of pasture and parcels of woodland which chase the valley bottom. 10 miles long, one wide, this fertile vale is held between the imposing abruptness of the chalk ridge and the limestone slopes to the south. This is old terrain, the hedgerows, barns and houses have served generations, the scenery draws you in, you sense hidden stories at every turn.

Confining Swanage's eastern frontier is an attractive sweep of beach. The tide's ebb and flow leaves tasty sea snails or sprats tangled in seaweed for a dinosaur feast. Bullish cries echo over the relaxed scene, sharp beaks strike and off the dinosaurs dart, much to the surprise of the *Homo sapiens* who has lost a sandwich. Zen in action.

It has always been about eat, escape being eaten, breed avidly so the survivors continue your genes. The genetical anomalies which work will continue, these aberrations refine old species, creating a new range of creatures. Roughly 120 million years ago, a small tree-living sub-species of the bounteous dinosaur group of animals developed feathers on the gangly arms reaching to their long fingered hands. Today their beaks, claws and caws display astonishing flying skills. If in doubt, next time you are at the coast, watch a crafty streetwise seagull stream in to snap up your neighbour's seaside snack.

120 mya

Every living creature harvests its surroundings and we humans are masters. A local limestone coffin dating from 2,800 years ago was found at Langton Matravers. Since Roman times this hallowed region has made good money from its geology - a panel of local 'marble' found in St Albans near London dates from the year 79.

Defining the south side of the valley, you'll notice the afore mentioned limestone ridge which parallels Ballard Down's continuity. It contains two subtly different rock types (actually, there's several, which is true for all simplified classifications herein). The bulk is Purbeck limestone formed in shallow lagoons which covered this region before the chalks you've walked were laid on top. We really are walking back through time.

Streaking west from Peveril Point on the seaward edge of Swanage, there's a thin seam of the highly prized Purbeck 'marble' - a faux term. Fresh water snail shells give the rock subtle colour variations and it polishes well. This luxuriant stone was sought-after in medieval times, however, working it required great skill and Corfe was the only 'marbling' (carving) centre outside London - Richard II's tomb in Westminster Abbey was constructed in 1400 from Purbeck 'marble'. Widely used for columns, pillars and sculptures it is in cathedrals such as Westminster and Salisbury as well as our grandest buildings. Locally, St James' Church in Kingston has columns, decorations and moulds of 'marble' which contrast with the pale Portland stone walls and arches. However, when used outside, the damp conditions crumble the muddy surroundings of the long gone fresh water snails, nonetheless, Purbeck 'marble' is still heavily quarried by several small outfits.

Where have those wonderful chalks which once overlaid this valley gone? Gone with the wet stormy wind, eroded by gales, millions of years of them gradually denuding the once solid landscape. This happens again and again, land is laid down then taken away, yet some places somehow retain some of the top strata. Confusing. But producing interesting landscapes, for each rock weathers at different speeds.

This brings us to the less amazing but still attractive and much stronger Purbeck limestone. Limestone's level strata is easy to split by hammering in chisels and wedges, consequently for thousands of years limestone has created iconic structures such as the Egyptian and Aztec pyramids. Here it's been widely used in local houses and manors.

From Swanage to a little beyond Worth Matravers, this reliable building material was quarried by small groups of men. They hauled it out of the many pits littering the area with ponies walking in circles around a capstan*.

Some of the most dramatic sites are Windspit and Seacombe on the cliffs below Worth Matravers. At these places the blocks were loaded onto small rowing boats which lugged these impossible loads through the rolling swell to waiting ships. It was a dangerous business frequently ending in accidents.

* a post turned by poles which pulls up a loaded rope

Eastwards along the northern slopes of this ridge, quarries at Langton Matravers had horses pulling carts along a tramway which ran to Swanage's fishing port. The town quickly grew as demand increased from expanding Victorian cities. Even in the harbour the hefty rock was loaded onto rowing boats, thence on to swaying ships until a pier was erected in 1860. London expanded with Purbeck limestone and returning ships brought as ballast, unwanted monuments removed from the capital.

This has given Swanage the nickname 'Little London by the Sea'. The town has the capital's discarded bollards, arches, obelisks, memorials, statues, even a weather vane from Billingsgate Market and there's a complete London building reassembled as the town hall. This was all thanks to John Mowlem, a local man and founder of the famous construction firm, as well as his nephew George Burt. For a bit of fun, there's a lively web-guide of these oddities, type in - Little London by the Sea and go to the londonist.com link.

The bounteous Victorian economy gave the ordinary person spare money and from 1830, workers were granted holidays. Until then, only pilgrims or the wealthy travelled without intention to work as or where they went. Swanage is a burst of holiday energy, artisanal ice creams, superb sand sculptures, tourist boats and timeless summer joy and this attracted boat loads of day trippers from Poole and Bournemouth. In 1897, a longer pier was opened, bringing 10,000 visitors during its first season. In 1940 part of the pier was blown up in fear that the Nazi might use it to take a foothold on the Isle of Purbeck. The structure was quickly rebuilt once peace arrived but the last paddle steamer delivering tourists to the pier was in 1966.

After 30 years of deterioration, a trust formed to maintain the edifice, which today requires a staggering £200,000 annually, even with the help of volunteer labour. Work without pay makes us feel part of a community, altruism also makes us feel better about ourselves, for we know we are giving without seeking reward.

As you leave the town maybe licking a fine local ice cream, ease yourself into the lush gardens created in 1996. There is no rush. The rushing has long been left behind, this is your treat to yourself. Let the flowers fill your lungs, the birdsong bing your heart, the leaves lick your finger tips and the mown grass bounce your step.

A little way along, at Durlston Bay's slumping cliffs, in 1857 the remarkable Samuel Beckles, a man with a fossil in his bonnet, undertook a dig with 100 paid navvies. He subsequently produced one of the finest fossil records of early mammals. Don't get too excited, our various forebears at this stage were tiny reptiles that looked vaguely like chunky cardboard model beasts from a 1950's filmset. Soon, well 5 million soons later, a minuscule ancestor of placental mammals arrived to dodge through dinosaur claws, these were ratty little things with attitude whose ancient ancestors had already survived the Triassic Extinction of 210 million years ago.

Evolution is amazing. Natural selection in Europe favoured pink skin for absorbing more vitamin D from the weaker sunshine, slowly rejecting beautiful dark skin. This process began just 10-13,000 years ago so it is easy to see that over the past 200 million years the clunky rodent's cousin became you!

Can we trust all this seeming baloney - that we evolved from ancient oddities that don't look anything like us? Turn the page and we'll briefly start at the… start.

the greatest fluke

Send your mind back 4,000 million, or 4 billion years.

At this time simple lifeforms thrived. Nothing gigantic, just microscopic species of bacteria and archaea (oddly, viruses are not considered to be 'alive'). This was either in shallow lagoons or perhaps deep in the ocean where broiling gases from the earth's centre spewed through bubbling vents at the edge of tectonic plates. Move on to 2.2 billion years ago and in that critical environment a type of archaea which had a nucleus decided to cuddle a hydrogen-eating bacteria called a mitochondria. This was an unusual move. Normally everything gobbled everything. These cuddling cells became such good pals that they stayed enjoined, protecting themselves with a membrane to contain their newly combined genetic material and information.

Eureka ! = Eurika-yote?

        No,   Eukar-**y**ote   *(U kar yote)*

As if that is not mind-blowing enough, genetic mutation created a fluke, these new eukaryotes worked out how to multiply!

     That is phenomenal.... Until that moment
bacteria, archaea and viruses multiplied by cloning
(and still do).

The eukaryote population exploded. Because things often went wrong, the uncertainties of genetic distortions created new life forms. The freaks which survived responded to specific environments, so evolving in different, ever more complex ways, triggering a revolution on steroids - cells simply can't stop themselves from experimenting (mutating).

another wonder

Each species was and is unique. With the tough process of natural selection and survival of the fittest, weeny wee worms without skeletons eventually emerged, they became a myriad of shapes and species and after millions of years of experimental merges, with such things as sea snails manifesting along the way, fish arrived, then fungi, plants, insects. Soon certain reptiles became dinosaurs and others, boom, begat mammals, then some slunk into the sea.

We can trace our lineage so far back and so clearly because the brighter sparks amongst us worked this out by looking at the evolutionary changes recorded in neatly interlinked cellular histories found in fossils around the world. Those evolving antediluvian patterns continue in all creatures and plants. Don't feel too comfortable, this euphoric lineage includes slime.

Living things are programmed to compete and everything eats another thing, yet we (non-bacterial, non-archaea), eukaryote species evolved due to the cooperation of two cells which, for a magical moment, opted out of the feast.

Eukaryotes are still with us - they're the basic complex cell in every tree, limpet and laughing child.
They collaborated, they evolved.

Humans are also capable of finding common ground and progressing from competitive beasts into creatures capable of discerning a lighter way forwards.

a canoeist passes Black Zawn caves
sea-cut into the bulk of Purbeck limestone

the limestone bulk

Further down the path lies Durslton Country Park, which George Burt of 'stones-to-London' fame magnanimously created to educate his townsfolk. It surrounds his ostentatious Victorian manor and, if you have the time, linger and discover the current interpretation of his legacy.

This limestone terrain is where our walk first encounters dinosaur remains. They were alive in chalky Cretaceous times, but conditions in the rocks weren't right for most fossilisation processes. Set down 140 million years ago, these more solid Purbeck limestone beds are rich in dinosaur tracks. Some footprints over one metre wide were plonked down by beasts besides which bull African elephants would look infantile. Upon the ridge above, at Keates Quarry which lies between the two Matravers, you can visit over 100 dinosaur tracks made by giant sauropods decorate strata laid down in steamy swamps and lagoons.

As if that's not enough, stepping up a wall inside Langton Matraver's Ship Inn are more dinosaur footsteps which are well worth a pint of cider. In 1878, poor old John Ball, then landlord of the Ship, was 'buried like a dog' beside the highway on a chilly December night. Suffering from depression after his estranged wife Mary had refused to return to him, he shot himself and was thus not permitted to be laid in consecrated ground. In those days such things mattered, so the good man was set to be eternally tempted by Old Harry and his demons.

140 mya

This upset the vicar who, preferring angels to devils, undertook a campaign which generated two Acts of Parliament and in 1888 suicide victims were allowed to have churchyard burials. Whee, the saints would look after John Ball forever. As might your sipping that cider in his old pub.

Talking of drink, smugglers once concealed kegs of brandy in Langton Matravers' 14th-century St George's Church. One of them, Charles Hayward, who in 1879 died aged 83, moved from dealing in contraband to becoming parish clerk, sub-postmaster, churchwarden and sexton, which proves that the pillars of society have always been fluid and have often had questionable beginnings. It's who you know…. More soberly, near the church stands a fine sculpture of a Purbeck quarryman, created by Mary Spencer Watson.

To its seaward side, Langton Matravers village is sheltered from the prevailing south-west winds by Purbeck's solid limestone ridge. Down beside the High Street, a line of 'Celtic', pre-Saxon fields prove this mile long settlement was here before the Roman Conquest, which the discovery of Celtic coins underscores. The Matravers family who later owned Langton and Worth Matravers, but lived just north of Poole Harbour in Lytchett Matravers, were originally called Montrauers and had arrived with the Norman invasion. One Matravers held Edward II prisoner before he was murdered in 1327 because this King was deemed unfit to rule, having lost Scotland, Ireland and Gascony. Fair cop, but death? Edward has proven a dodgy name for our monarchs, three out of eleven being killed, one abdicating and two got heavily involved in troubling warfare.

As you continue along the coastal path, if the tide is right, there's a superb optical illusion to be enjoyed at Dancing Ledge. When this flat area of rock at the base of a small cliff is washed by rolling waves the movement makes the submerged ledge appear to bop.

Purbeck stone was quarried here and the ledge proved perfect for small ships to dock against. This also made it an easy landing spot for smugglers, though today the surrounding cliffs are popular with climbers. There's also a small rock pool suitable for swimming, yet do not be tempted to swim in the sea. Here currents are strong and unpredictable, beware too of rock hopping, waves have plucked fit folk from these cliffs.

Pick up a chunk of limestone - is it heavy? Explore its attributes, sensing its temperature, firmness, texture with the senses you inherited from lizards. Trapped in this stone are the remains of creatures long forgot, as one day will we be. Today is precious, treasuring its every hour is greater than treasure.

Not far around the corner in this zone of grey solidity that has withstood millennia of raging storms, lies one of the most artistic of beacons. Anvil Lighthouse built in 1881 boasted a significant new design. Doing away with reflective prisms to magnify light, it used dense flint glass for the lens, sending out a powerful beam easily seen across 19 miles of waves. Even without spectacles, the average human eye, on a clear calm night can detect the light of a single candle at that distance!

Sight developed in primitive worms as cells which perceive changes in light. Gradually these became crude lenses which spotted objects without registering definition, and then came the first rounded lens which could capture an image. Over millions of years of trial and error, the survivors carried these improving lenses until fish grew films protecting the feature from salt water. Certain dinosaur-period creatures who had eyes, such as the pliosaur, retained those primitive sensors as a 'third-eye', as do a few creatures today, the crocodile being one.

Our human eye is one of our many links to the reptilian proto-dinosaurs from which we mammals evolved. Our brain reacts instantly to changes in light and movement, yet our human eye has no need to be as sharp as an eagle's, leaving the brain to give more attention to our sensitive hands. Yet the brain is still programmed to respond to movement before anything else, even before messages arriving from our precious finger tips and wild minds.

Anvil Lighthouse

Tilly Whim caves

Below Anvil Lighthouse lie Tilly Whim caves. The caverns from which limestone was excavated are clearly visible from the path, as is the ledge from which the weighty loads were lowered to rowing boats… it makes you shiver.…

You would by now have noticed the coastline's shape changes due to the sea's play against rock types. The weaker sands of Studland, and Swanage's sand and muds, produce curved bays, whilst the solid stuff such as these limestones produce near straight lines dented by local weakness. Storms speeding in from the Atlantic have snipped away at fissures in these solid cliffs, expanding them, leaving a string of mysterious caves only canoeists can enjoy. One such crack has formed a blowhole which spurts sea swell into the air, but do leave these features to be seen by the seals, unless you are with experts.

A little out from this inspiring coastline sharks, whales and an abundance of fish inhabit waters where huge British fishing fleets once worked. This marine wealth was why, during the madness of Brexit, European countries fought not to let go of the fishing rights which Britain had handed out when first entering the EU in1973. That trade-in killed our fishing fleets, shattering centuries old fishing communities. There had been over-fishing, granted, but this was exacerbated by EU fleets whose governments granted easy subsidies and loans, inspiring large, aggressively industrial fleets with sophisticated equipment. Unaided, the remaining British fishermen struggled to compete. Around the world finely balanced marine ecosystems are threatened by decades of irresponsible harvesting, but today, in certain protected areas depleted species are slowly recovering.

the Square and Compass pub

a worthy villager

Up atop the broad limestone ridge sits Worth Matravers, where a huge quarry still exploits limestone, though the village is surrounded by arable and pasture land. An incredible 74% of Britain's surface is farmed, in Japan this is only 12%, whilst France uses 52%. However, France's favourable weather and terrain means she exports vast quantities of her products and is Europe's only member of the short list of self sufficient countries, food wise, handy in an over populated world competing for limited resources.

One of the main reasons humanity has thrived so well lies in Worth's graveyard. A farmer called Benjamin Jesty, who, when he lived in Yetminster near Yeovil invented vaccination almost thirty years before Edward Jenner, the man 'famed' for this innovation. In the 1700's, smallpox killed 400,000 Europeans annually. Jesty noticed that dairymaids who got cowpox seemed not to get smallpox so he rubbed pus from infected udders into scratches he made in his family's arms and they easily survived a local outbreak of cowpox. Years later his two boys failed to catch an outbreak of the far more serious smallpox. Yet locals saw him as inhuman and Jesty was, "Hooted at, reviled and pelted whenever he attended market," according to a Yetminster neighbour.

That may well have prompted the family's move to Worth Matravers in 1797, just as Jenner spread vaccination worldwide. Dr Andrew Bell, rector of Swanage, documented Jesty's work and subsequently vaccinated 200 of his parishioners. In 1805 Jesty was finally given wider recognition and was invited to the Vaccine Pock Institute in London, where his eldest son survived being inoculated with live smallpox. His resilience was 'proven', though Jesty had had no doubts thirty years previously.

The institute presented Jesty with a testimonial scroll, expenses and fittingly, two ceremonial gold lancets, (items used to scratch the skin). They also paid for a portrait which in 2006 the Wellcome Trust bought to hang in their London headquarters. "We should all draw inspiration from the ingenuity and courage of this humble (and portly) Dorset (farmer)," wrote Patrick Pead, a retired microbiologist and author of 'Benjamin Jesty: the Grandfather of Vaccination.'

Smallpox killed millions; it was finally eradicated worldwide in 1979, the only infectious disease to then be snuffed out. A man I knew was key to this programme in India, where smallpox had been rife.

Jetsy might have enjoyed the collection of inspiring ciders on offer in the village's atmospheric pub. Local, even organic, an unindustrialised treat meaning that your money will end up here rather than in London. Our Civil War introduced West Country cider to the wider country. The Square and Compass opened four years before Jesty arrived in the village and has more recently been run by the same family for over 100 years. The pub, which has a small museum with fossils and local artefacts, holds an annual stone carving festival.

On the headland there's a Coast Watch Station manned by volunteers watching out for the safety of sailors and walkers. There's also an artful sculpture signalling the British development of radar, for Worth Matravers had one of the cliff-top chain of radar stations which proved decisive in the allied victory over the Nazis. Radar was one of the many extraordinary inventions which this outstandingly inventive country has given away over the decades.

The Americans were reluctant to help Britain restock her dwindling arms stock. However, Henry Tizard's August 1940 mission to Washington changed this - "The most valuable cargo ever brought to our shores," exclaimed the director of the US Office of Strategic Services. Tizard's pile of unique research documents were on: radar technology, atom-bomb research, a turbojet engine, automatically timed bombs, anti-aircraft and anti-tank weapons, rockets, gun sights, chemical weapons, plastic explosives, sonar and gyroscopic gunsights.

This prompted the USA in 1941, to finally replenish our diminishing munitions, but at a huge price. Even having given our secrets freely, Britain was only able to pay off this vast debt in 2007, when Gordon Brown, Chancellor of the Exchequer, ceremoniously left 11 Downing Street with a briefcase full of... documents? No, dosh.

Standing above all such tales of history, upon an impressive bulk projecting into the sea, stands a Norman Chapel built on an earlier chapel which might have been somewhere to pray for those who drowned in the dangerous waters off St Aldhelm's Head. Nearby, a slab two metres long with a Celtic cross stood above a 40 year old woman's grave. It is now to be found in Worth Matravers' church.

She must have been important to have had such attention. Who was this long forgotten woman? Our little histories so soon lost, yet when alive so vibrant, which makes one wish our days were well spent.

Rounding the limestone butt of St Aldhelm's Head, you notice the predictable limestone has thinned to mere icing atop messy lumps of slumping strata. These are the Kimmeridge shales and clays. Here you dip into a sudden vale where an ancient torrent once carved a deep gouge that pierced the limestone cap to slice deep through the softer clay-stone.

This dell reaches back from the inviting jewel of Chapman's Pool which is encased in tumbling slopes. If you are in need of a dip and the weather is clement, the Pool is a safe bet. If not, perhaps walk with the ghosts of smugglers to rise through the steep vale. When chased, those hardened folk would have stolen inland up the stream trickling through this charmed and secret gully, to sneak away into one of five dry little depressions cut into the capping.

Chapman's Pool and vale

intellectual superstars

As you keep noticing, the land often buckles and twists. Strange, when all that sedimentary laying was a flat affair. Well, a quick lesson in soup geology might help.

Hold tight.
Our beloved Earth is akin to a boiling projectile of thick lentil soup jiggling in space's freezing environment. Upon cooling, this delicious orb formed an outer scab that is always shifting (incredibly slowly) due to convectional currents rising from deep within our bubbling centre. These hidden forces shift and wrinkle the apparently solid continents we inhabit.

There we are,
plate tectonics
in a soupçon.

Now that you know how this land was lifted, tilted and sliced about, do a little skip for having increased your brain power... the act of skipping flashes another lightbulb.
But whoever thought this out?
Whilst we napped flint in our caves, the concept might well have germinated as part of our aforementioned fascination with stone. Early man was intelligent, but to conjure up these complicated geological theories? Even with today's finger-tip internet, geology is a tough topic to unpick.

The first recorded step came from a wise Greek named Xenophanes, who described fossil fish and shells in 540BC. Two hundred years later, Aristotle wrote 'Mineralogy and Meteorology', which a Persian called Ibn Sina refined roughly

1,300 years later. In that same medieval period, the Indian Abu al-Rayhan al-Biruni, proclaimed his country had once been under a sea. Their Chinese contemporary Shen Kuo, finding petrified moisture-loving bamboo in China's dry north, wrote a theory on climate change. Shen Kuo went on to described the process of land formation based on finding fossil shells hundreds of miles from the ocean, and thence declared that landscapes are shaped by the erosion of mountains and the subsequent deposition of silt.

That is smart.

Europeans were still arguing that God's Great Biblical Flood had configured rock strata within a Flat Earth, though Old Harry might have disagreed. Strangely, it was a bishop (beatified in 1988) called Nicolas Steno, who in 1659 questioned the European notion that fossils grew in the ground. In 1741, a period when the Church stated the Earth was about 5,000 years old, France's National Museum of Natural History created the world's first geology teaching position. Forty years later, geology was unified as a theory by a Scot called James Hutton who said the Earth was a molten mass (with volcanic processes), upon whose cooling surface base rocks formed. Hey presto - soup geology.

Let's wrap this up by reeling back to when Africa rudely bumped into Europe. Tectonics in action, ruffling the Alps, rumpling these chalk and limestone ridges along with much else which lies beneath.

oil & co

The breath flies with the arresting line of rises and dips defining this coast. Relish this exercise for opening up your airways, thus helping to add extra time to your life. Puffing and rising to the limestone chunk of Houns Tout, you'll arrive at a perfect spot to honour the dead - as the ancient mounds up here reveal. The views are stupendous. What a moment of joy!

The path continues without touching a settlement for what will become over eighteen miles since Swanage, quite a distance without a shop in this crowded little country. This gives the illusion that you are beyond humanity's heavier touch. Enjoy it. Forget that during the past three decades of unbridled economic expansion the natural world has altered more than it had since the last Ice Age. Let nature replenish your heart here amongst wild flowers, buzzing bees and butterflies, this slender haven where anthropic space meets what was once our limit - the wild sea.

Beneath Houns Tout, by the slate cliffs of Egmont Bight, you'll hear a waterfall! A rare splash of surface water since Swanage Bay tumbles from hidden fish ponds enclosed in the wooded world of Encombe House, a secret step up this secluded valley. Be cautious, however tempting a track might be, if it's not a public footpath set one toe upon our land and we English feel imposed upon. Once in Europe, woken at dawn by a tractor I apologised for accidentally parking the night in a private farmyard; the chuckling farmer also apologised for waking me and he offered me breakfast!

12,000 y a

Our strong sense of private space, which includes a tight aura surrounding our bodies, probably arises from living on a grey, windy-wet and crowded little rock. Some argue that the organised Normans, whose 1086 Doomsday survey recorded every inch and item owned from chicken to haywain to shed, lead to such individualism, for we are less collectivist, more protective.

Even today many a Norman rule persists. Home owners collectively assume they own 4.5% of England (that does not include the vast estates), but we merely rent our minute specks of land from the crown. Furthermore, the continuity of a monarch rather than an ever changing president, influences our top-down social structure. The Norman upper classes worked assiduously to maintain their privileges and French was considered superior. Essential even until the 1980's amongst the elite and the highly educated, (my mother was fluent). French people have told me, "English is French badly pronounced," but today's English is a complex mix of Celtic/German/Latin with Norman-French tossed on top. This feisty lot provided a rich cultural base which is constantly enhanced by newly arriving cultures.

In common with many estates across this country, Encombe dates from long before the Norman conquest; unlike most, it wasn't taken over by them because the church owned it. Upon dissolving the monasteries in 1536, Henry VIII sold Encombe but 16 years later the estate passed back to the government when the owner, Sir Thomas Arundel was beheaded by Edward VI. Those Edwards... It has been sold four more times since and the present owner bought the estate from the Earl of Eldon for a tidy sum in 2009.

There's another ancient estate on the bulky ridge above, which owns much of Kimmeridge. The landlord, Philip Mansel, a direct descendant of William Wyot who bought Smedmore estate more than 600 years ago, is an* historian with many acclaimed books to his name. His ancestors made jewellery and, oddly, furniture from Kimmeridge shale found on the family's privately owned beach. The Romans also used a version of the rock, burnt red, for ornamental flooring.

From the organic content in the shales, the family extracted gas which lit the romantic city of Paris in the 1800's. Down on the beach a nodding donkey has kept pumping out oil since 1961. Though currently gurgling forth 60 barrels a day, providing a daily revenue equivalent to more than the average monthly salary in SW England, it is a far cry from the family's 350 daily barrels in an epoch when CO_2's effects were not widely accepted.

Cutting the use of these warming gases is vital. Finding a route to sustainability which doesn't harm the fragile balance between wealth, hence taxes and need, which is met by those taxes, is a puzzle.

This fuel seeps up from inter-connected reserves 350 metres underground and which extend 5 miles out to sea. These come from Carboniferous strata created by decaying jungle mulch long before big-footed dinos were even thought of, at a time when reptiles and huge insects dominated. 220 million years ago, most land was enjoined in a hot, dry super-block called Pangea. As Pangea split apart roughly between 250-190 million years ago, around the new continents' edges lagoons and shallows were formed. These cooler, welcoming environments generated an explosion of species as successful genetic aberrations produced creatures which evolved to fill ecological gaps.

300 mya

201-170 mya

*for example, using 'an' before 'h' is an Anglo-French habit, because 'h' is softly pronounced

The clays here contain fossils, but you can't remove them from this private beach. Talking of fossils, there's a modern day Mary Anning (the wondrous fossil lady of Lyme Regis) who has a world acclaimed museum amongst Kimmeridge village's attractive homes. The remarkable Dr Steve Etches, a local plumber with at least seven species named after him, was fascinated by his first find, a sea urchin down on Kimmeridge beach when he was an infant (Mary Anning also started as a child, it must be a Dorset thing).

His extraordinary collection of late Jurassic creatures eventually filled his garage and when he attracted world-wide interest, he moved them to an artfully constructed museum, assisted by the Mansel family, as well as funding from the National Lottery. The Etches Collection is a beautiful museum containing world firsts in ammonite eggs, as well as an icthyosaur with a belly full of fish and squid. There is also one of the best preserved heads of a pliosaur, at over 2 metres in length it illustrates how large sea reptiles got before their extinction. Superbly cleaned over 18 months, it is a unique gem. This sketch with its minute human figures illustrates

extracting the pliosaur

the danger of extracting the complete head from half way up a crumbling cliff near Kimmeridge. We will lightly* touch on these wondrous creatures when we get to Charmouth and Lyme Regis.

* it's not my place to compete with all those excellent dinosaur & geology books....

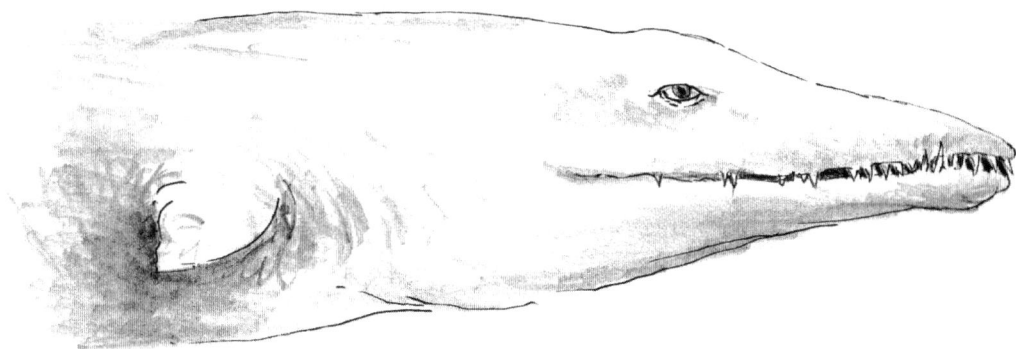

Imagine the stress of meeting one of these magnificent creatures as you swam across Weymouth Bay! That's when our flight or flight stress response kicked in. Life today is differently stressful, it is in our heads and so we need a remedy that doesn't involved pelting away from huge jaws. The way out is easy, but requires commitment.

Take a minute to enjoy your body breathing easily without your interference. Relish the unforced inflow of life-giving oxygen; relax as it flows out naturally. That's all. Switch off your phone. Start it early each morning as you sit in the bathroom, the kitchen, again each time you have a few seconds. Once more a spurt at work, another waiting for the bus, as you walk the streets, back watching the kettle boil, after your evening shower. What a treat this elegantly powerful little pleasure.

Dr Steve Etches' pliosaur

danger, flying bullets... only walk
the 8 miles between Kimmeridge & Lulworth when ammunition isn't popping the ranges surrounding this iconic area. Even summer weekends can be shell-hell! Red flags + locked gates declare days alive with feisty troops. When permitted, to avoid ghosting yourself, keep to the paths, stay within the marked zones.

A step too far, boom.

LOOK at

https://www.gov.uk/government/publications/lulworth-firing-notice/lulworth-range-firing-times

not lipstick

to tyneham

Recorded as a goat enclosure in the 1086 Doomsday Book, since WW2, Tyneham has trained troops. Resting amongst shells, preserved by gunpowder, the hamlet takes you back in time. Dear Mr Bond who in 1943 was forced to hand over the land his family had owned for centuries, died of a broken heart when the military refused to give it back after the war, rendering 225 villagers homeless. Tyneham, a village in aspic, is worth a visit should you wish to sense a little of what life looked like in the 1930's. Ian Fleming, who went to school locally, borrowed one of Bond's ancestors who had spied for England four centuries before, namely James Bond.

If you are interested, the world's first tank was tested not far away at Bovington in 1916, where lies the most important collection of military tanks worldwide. Was the Trojan Horse the first tank, a concept Leonardo da Vinci revived when he redrew other people's tank illustrations?

Sadly, armies must protect us from aggressors. Such has been the scheme of things since the beginning - each pathogen, complex cell and wiggling creature struggling to survive life's *everything-eat-everything* feast, has to fight its corner.

Our present military forces use interesting techniques. I once saw crack SAS troops doing yoga after a run. Moreover, to maintain calm when things go pop, troops learn to de-stress with breathing that triggers the parasympathetic nervous system, whose vagus nerve controls involuntary functions such as your heart rate.

That stress can deeply inhibit soldiers is
obvious. When swimming across winter
rivers, a simple technique prevents
individuals from gasping, panicking and
drowning. Slow, attentive deep
breathing slows the heartbeat,
eases high blood pressure,
changes the perception of pain.
This affects the vagus nerve.
Alert to beneficial inflowing
oxygen, slowly breathe in,
expanding the lungs. Hold and
appreciate your remarkable
being. Slowly let go as you feel
yourself relaxing. This walk could
help you habituate this easy procedure
which should help you face life's inevitable
tensions.

Crows hop about, pecking at insects, digging for worms, they rise to shoo off lapwings, magpies and other hungry birds. They will clock your voice and face, if you are a regular they'll recognise your return. Should you be afraid or aggressive, they will respond accordingly.

Round a corner or two from Kimmeridge, you rise 137 metres from Brandy Bay, which speaks well for French produce and the smuggling crowds. Surmounting the bulk of Purbeck limestone, below your toes lies Tyneham. The ridge sinks into Worbarrow Bay, taking with it the thin seam of faux marble which began at Peveril Point. These strata terminate as the cheeky little snout called Worbarrow Tout.

If sure-footed, do climb this oddly named 50m knoll of Purbeck stone and 'marble' to walk carefully about its top. Should the tide be low, from Worbarrow beach you can clamber over rocks beneath the Tout and thank the Jurassic Coast for a clear splay of slices of strata plunging from a shallow to a steep angle into the water. You can explore such features even more with Google Earth. On a more terrestrial note, tucked under Tout's eastern armpit lies the quaintest miniature bay.

A kilometre from Tyneham, this is the end of the fertile valley at whose far end lies monument-filled Swanage. You may wish for a swim before tackling the impressive hill ahead that runs to Old Harry. Again you trudge up chalky Cretaceous slopes to the narrow ridge whose sharp drop to the north and plunge to the sea are arresting.

From up here, the vastness of the scene stills the mind, awe kicks in. Linger with this graceful humility, sinking it through your brain, forming an enriching mindset into which you can slip from time to time. Comprehending without thought the stupendous immensity of existence, we sense we are part of it and we know our duty is to tread as lightly as we can.

Upon this imposing 170m summit lies the Iron Age fort of Flower's Barrow. These ramped up ramparts are slipping towards the sea as the waves crumble the long cliff below, revealing the pace of coastal erosion over the past 2,500 years. All about here there's an abundance of ancient burial mounds and in the wider region there are a number of late Bronze Age and Iron Age forts. The latter were marketplaces but also strongholds for those living in the valleys.

The Celts are likely to have spread out from Poole Harbour, avoiding the densely wooded valleys and swampy Frome by walking along this open ridge reaching back to Corfe. Along came their dogs, semi-domesticated pigs and cattle; tiny creatures like the dormouse arrived with the barley and oats brought over from Europe and Turkey. Incredibly, by the first century BC, the local Durotriges tribe exported grain to Rome, showing how well organised they were. They minted their own coins and these have been found in Brittany, with whom they also traded.

Julius Caesar stopped such activity when he invaded Brittany in 56 BC, because he preferred working with the people of Essex. Rising population on top of years of soil abuse (what's new?), meant locals here were malnourished by 43 CE, which made the Roman conquest of Dorset an easy task.

The first clans who arrived after the ice retreated have left their mark in the people of Dorset and Somerset. DNA tests show that a significant proportion are directly descended from those original immigrants. Today Britain feels over-crowded, people wish for our population to stop expanding, forgetting that we have always been a nation of immigrants.

Fittingly for a hill fort, the slopes of Flower's Barrow still shiver with the modern equivalent of clattering sabres. They did so way back in 1678 when the local landlord, his brother and four workmen heard the clanking armour of walking soldiers as well as the noises of accompanying horses. It is claimed that 100 villagers spotted this phantom army. In desperation, a messenger was sent to warn the people in Wareham of impending danger; that it never arrived raised embarrassing questions in Parliament.

This ghostly army reappeared in the 1930's. Not so long ago on Binden Hill near Lulworth, somebody spotted a cruder clan clad in skins. Perhaps a lost group of Glastonbury ravers?

Chuckle. Laughter, they have found, even if forced, jiggles more than your eyelashes, it spins teasing serotonin, the happiness hormone, into your brain....

You are back amongst the flints. To celebrate, bend down and select a tool. As you hold this solid ally of humanity, imagine yourself being alone in the starkness of nature without any modern trappings. Beneath our civilised veneer we retain the raw alertness of our Stone Age ancestors, find yourself in mortal danger and it should kick in. We also have many prehuman attributes - our most inner brain, the amygdala, a kernel atop the spine, developed before dinosaurs existed. It instinctually reacts and is in continual alertness, so lingers on the verge of anxiety. When disoriented, such apprehension spreads to our minds.

The amygdala is capped by a mammalian brain, developed when dangerous dinosaurs were about. Surrounding these is the neocortex whose basis was created when we primarily hung about in trees forming complex social bonds. This is fronted by the outstanding prefrontal cortex that evolved as climate change opened out the grassy savannah. Adapting, we learnt to hunt and then hide in clumps of trees and shrubs. We had to refine ape-ish language, develop rationality, reasoning and abstract thinking alongside complex memories and planning. Oh, plus developing labyrinthine selves with dazzling ego games which helped us find our place in the complexity of the tribal pecking order.

Learning to sense which characteristic we find ourselves 'in' as we respond to the world is a useful skill. This trail which traces the evolution of one third of life on Earth can help us upgrade the way we travel through each day's challenges.

Durdle storm

lulworth

Hidden in the chalky folds, away from the confounded confusion of manoeuvring tanks and flashing guns, stands the well proportioned Lulworth Castle. Built in Elizabethan times, owned for over 400 years by the Weld family, it sits amidst twenty square miles of beautiful landscape which includes Durdle Door and Lulworth Cove. That is a staggering 4 by 5 miles, roughly 7 by 8 kilometres; there are over 3,000 such estates in this fair land.

William the Conquerer repaid his invading Norman soldiers with land (also eternally rented from him). That was about 7,000 families, some received huge estates, others manor houses and farms. Many families with anglicised French names have lived in the same spot since that time. Near me the same family have inhabited their property since 1087. Today 1% of our population owns 64% of this country, 47% of that belongs to our gentry and aristocracy, 17% to the nouveau riche. Contextualising this, all environmental charities, which includes the huge National Trust, own just 2%.

It's amusing to ask: had we inherited such estates, what would we have done? Tarnish the rolling hills with hotels or theme parks, as has happened. Would we be better served by donating all this to publicly owned charities such as the Trust, as have several aristocratic families? We might, as have the owners of Knepp Castle in Kent, have shown that careful re-wilding can create an acclaimed ecological haven.

It must be stated that aristocratic land is frequently richer in wildlife and less polluted than commercial farms (whose terrain these families often own and rent out). For example, the Isle of

Purbeck, which has its share of private estates, boasts Britain's greatest number of wild flowers, counting the early spider orchid amongst them.

To the Weld's credit, whilst cows on their fields produce 25 million litres of milk annually, whilst munitions fly about and tourists' cars flood in, they look after their terrain with admirable sensitivity. Their variety of habitats contain over 60% of British butterfly species, including their very own - the Lulworth Skipper.

And so to the perfect cove. Created by a goddess craving a retreat within which to rest her soul and enchant humanity forever and add glory to a beautifully varied coastline. Blame those two ridges, chalk and limestone streaking here from Old Harry's toes and Swanage's nose. Meeting and greeting, carved by waves, they formed an oval haven. Don't be surprised, you had a sneak preview at Worbarrow Bay. The limestones there did a sea-dip and it rose again at Mupe Bay to flow here. Zillions of waves pierced this rampart, gouging out Lulworth Cove.

What an ecosystem nature provided for our distant ancestors, with fungi and herb-rich wooded slopes, a fresh chalk stream filled with trout and shrimps weaving back from this secret bay. A sheltered cove with its harvest of molluscs, mackerel and sea bream, the old tumuli and barrows adorning these elegant slopes show how well they loved Lulworth.

As time rolled on, Purbeck's medieval squires and their families demanded labour from the people their surfs, which could either be a good life or a disaster depending on the landlord's character. Taxed too heavily as the elite consumed the best whilst expecting to have it at a decent price, it is no wonder seaside folk sought a trade which brought in extra money.

Lulworth - impression
from various sources

It was easy for fishermen to take aboard contraband from French or Channel Island sailors, who came from lands once owned by the English Normans. Land lubbers hauled it up the cliffs, locals and publicans hid it in their attics or cellars, carters lugged it inland, farmers stored the stash in their barns and traders in the nearest towns arranged deals with others who took it to cities such as Salisbury or London, thus ensuring that the profits were well distributed.

In the 1710's and 20's, the violent landlord of the Ship Inn at Wool ensured his contraband had a safe journey via a network of depots and carriers. There was the cunning smuggler of nearby Winfrith Newburgh who legitimately bought seized contraband and sold it onwards mixed with freshly smuggled items. If challenged, Charles Weeks showed duty-paid receipts, or he'd threaten officers with legal action, which no government worker could afford.

Lulworth's protected cove could be used in almost all weather conditions and village smugglers made a good living handling cocoa, brandy, coffee, lace and more. Upon the beach in the 1720's, smugglers fought off customs men for twelve hours before stealing away with as much wine and brandy as they could; afterwards, locals helped themselves to abandoned barrels.

The high stakes meant that both sides were pushed into violence. In the 1780's, customs officers fired canons at the beach as 20 tons of tea was unloaded. Most of the haul was taken away on government carts but it was later stolen from officials by force. In 1832 Lieutenant Edward Knight, a customs officer from Kent, was tossed over Durdle Door, his body lies in Weymouth graveyard.

Down at Mupe Bay lies the Smugglers' cave, which can only be approached when the tide is low. Inside this small natural feature contraband was hidden from prying eyes and protected from the waves by a solid wall. A mile east of Lulworth lies a cove called Airish Mell which was an ideal landing spot, and behind it lies a dry valley which curves inland in four confusing branches. Once five luggers unloaded at the same time, with countless people helping.

Such a superb location has attracted writers, poets, film stars and even academics such as Bertrand Russell, whose Linguistic Philosophy once entangled my illogical mind. And the incomers keep coming, you, me and all those cars which annually carry 500,000 visitors to this long-loved honeypot with its shops and eateries.

Lull upon the beach, remove your boots, let the wavelets splash your toes as you lazily head beyond the sunbathers. This enticing curve of nature is littered with fossilised sponges from tropical lagoons - the flints! Upon the cove's eastern sea-cliff lie rounded lumps of fossilised trees from the late Jurassic.

Down by the waves lies the tiny nook of Stair Hole. Two sea caves were pierced into the solid limestone and two old ones have collapsed to form open entrances through which the rampaging sea floods. The goddess was on absinthe as she flung the strata skywards. And the inner cliff has wildly contorted bands of rock. Blame Africa shunting into Europe during the Alpine orogeny 65 million years ago, tipping and twisting what had once been flat strata. You are allowed to shout, "Alpine Orogeny!" What art, accompanied by the restless pounding sea....

Atop Lulworth village stands Hambury Tout. From here you'll see that Old Harry's narrow chalky rush has suddenly expanded into a bundle of broad hills. Tectonic buckling of the chalk spreads north in a series of interconnected ranges whose valleys have been carved out by centuries of rainwater.

Water trickled through the chalk, hitting an impermeable strata, it seeped out sideways to create rare chalk streams, of which England has 160 of the world's stock of two hundred and ten. 60 million year old chalk aquifers give these streams clear pure water, enabling them to support a huge variety of species. Damselflies, mayfly and dragonflies feed trout, minnows, grayling, there are salmon and white-clawed crayfish for otters and kingfisher to eat, and so much more. Sadly, runoff chemicals from farming threatens such rare ecosystems.

Walking onwards you'll meet lenses from Tucson to Tokyo snapping Durdle Door from every angle. Quick, do a Durdle selfie for next time you come it'll have shrunk. Should technology allow you to live a few thousand years, this limestone magic which rushed from Worbarrow Tout, past Stair Hole where it did that flip upwards, will be gone. The Alpine orogeny hoiked these limestone strata upright, enabling gravity and storms to more easily pull apart the once level ramparts of strata and so carve this beautiful arch.

Either side of the Door the waves have created two elegant curved beaches into the softer chalks. If you're up for a chilly swim across the English Channel, you'll find these white chalks reappear in Normandy. Joking aside, be careful, the wave-tug is deep and powerful and currents swirling around the arch can be strong.

Late summer 2020, Covid lockdown eased. Vehicles filled the carparks, relieved crowds carrying heavy bags of grub delighted in being free. Having guzzled and gorged and gulped on Durdle Door beach, they chucked their light food wrappers to foul the superb spot they had scampered to see. We carry the heavy, discard the light. How absurd.

Making manufacturers accountable for the after-life of their products would help, for we are monkeys programmed by biodynamics to discard banana skins and let them rot, as our rubbish did before this age of disregard. The lush wrappings of many foods get as much creative attention as the industrialised food inside. Choosing products sustainably wrapped in biodegradable tissue will ensure our rubbish won't be here for thousands of years. Plastic wrappers and containers break down over hundreds, even thousands of years to form micro-plastics which now adorn every beach, field and mountain peak. Plastic junk despoils every shoreline around the entire world. But also, why not make your own picnic? Mankind's influence on ecosystems, climate and geology now outweighs nature's. Welcome to the age of the Anthropocene.

Shake such thoughts off with a dawdle west along Durdle's longer beach. The cliff of gleaming creams has artistically carved nodules, sea sculptured swirls, curly wave-worn weaves and all sorts of fine details scattered within its imposing facade. There's even a wave sculpted seat or two sunken into the chalk wall.

Enjoy the soft rock which resembles time hardened lime plaster. Run your hand, even your cheek over its smooth surface, igniting your senses, allowing your spirit to drift and forget time's ticking tug.

Time, economists tell us, is money. Not here, not right now. Time, if we wish, can be on our side as a magical orb into which we slip to lose ourselves and emerge later, refreshed.

If the waves aren't too wild and close, relax with the sea's majestic orchestrations. Relish the inter-weaving sounds, splashes and trills, the slushes and swirls, swooshes and splutters, one on top of the other. Nature's aural joy!

Durdle shedding gulls

to white nothe

And onwards we walk, floating with the gulls whilst the sea moves so far below as we rise and fall and up again to descend once more. Dips in the chalk atop the cliff which drops to infinity, one called Scratchy Bottom makes you wonder if a suicidal ancient tobogganist sped down on a skin which wore through....and the clifftops can be unstable! Rising and falling up these wave-truncated ridges and valleys, that's why they're called bottoms, your body will know you have achieved something.

Bat's Head does indeed look like a giant mammal peering out to sea. Atop its fragile protrusion, you'll also see that the chalk strata which is roughly horizontal along the clifftop suddenly goes batty and shoots vertically. The inspiring views are worth the balancing act, unless vertigo overwhelms you. Facing our fears shoots adrenaline through us, overcoming them, even slightly, hands us a dopamine award, as our fatally sledging forebear probably knew.

Looking back towards Durdle, you'll notice an older bat, well, more a baton, thinner than Harry's wife she stands alone in the water. If the sea is calm, you'll notice the sunken continuation of Durdle Door's solid strata whose remnants have been called - the Calf, Cow, Blind Cow and Bull... by farmers?

What a marvel, the sheer beauty of the rippling ridges devoid of villages, away from the buzz of traffic. Tranquillity, you all by yourself, how soothing.

100m above this pendulous cliff-path looms the ridge whose untreated seaward side enables up to 40 vegetal species to exist per square metre on the rare chalk grassland. Predictably, the plateau beyond is intensely arable and the odd tractor ploughs, sows or harvests. Trying to feed our densely populated little country, farmers turned to industrial farming, using heavy machinery, but that crushes the soil structure as well as its millions of vital mini creatures. Many are now trying to be more sustainable, but adjusting is a slow, difficult journey - most of their current takings are committed to expensive loans, leaving them with tiny rewards. The winners are the supermarkets, banks and agricultural suppliers. However, selling locally, some farmers are finding a more profitable and satisfying solution.

Above the looming bulk of White Nothe a row of old coastguard cottages is a reminder of the late 1800's when the government decided to get tough on smugglers, which, as we've seen, wasn't easy for both sides. Imagine what hard work tugging a net containing a barrel of brandy from Bordeaux up these cliffs and 'bottoms'. Forty, fifty pairs of hands, heels dug in to the crumbly earth, backs straining. Bridport rope no doubt. If you were caught it could be used as the 'Bridport Dagger' - slung around your neck by the laughing exercise men. Often supported by chuckling local landlords whom you had long supplied with smuggled delights, this elite who'd not so long stolen your right to graze common land. Such resentment fuelled the smugglers' strength and that brandy money certainly helped.

Stepping down from White Nothe's elevation, you come across a land change. Until now, you've been moving casually backwards in time through strata laid over millennia - the new Studland sands, those chalks, the limestones and beneath them all the

more ancient Kimmeridge shales; at
Lulworth you were in chalk again but
here, bang, without passing through
the limestones, you drop once more to
Kimmeridge. As if that's not confusing
enough, right across this low bay and to
the distant hills surrounding Abbotsbury, all
the layers which should be above your head
have been wiped away, devoured by millions of
years of storms which wore rocks to sand and washed it all down
to the seabed, (creating new strata).

These hills slightly inland are a patchwork of fields, copses and thickets, a feature which defines England's topography and which was instigated by Bronze Age man. Many land owners today are reviving a little of what was, 6-8,000 years ago, a forested island and nature immediately responds. I live next to an empty building plot which, every few years the owner cuts and sprays with poison. A year in the desert, then it bounces back. Wild flowers bring in insects, bushes attract small birds and slowly a delightfully dense scrubland adorns what staid eyes might see as an eyesore, but which to me is an ecological haven.

And so we walk on. We were made to walk. We were nomads following our prey, scuttling off to hunt, dashing to safety with our children. We strode across the Red Sea and peopled the world. It is only the last few generations of humanity who've been hooked into a sedentary existence and whilst sitting is the next cancer, walking pumps us up emotionally, mentally, physically.

What a refined instrument we keep stamping on. In each foot twenty six bones move thirty three joints; there's over one hundred muscles, tendons and ligaments arranged in three interacting arches - inner, outer and transverse. As you step down, these arches stretch and flex elastically, absorbing energy and as the foot rolls forward, transferring weight to our toes, up flicks the ankle as the tendons snap, exploding stored power into each step. The simple process of walking is, if you are attentive, utterly absorbing. Thank your fabulous feet for adding spring to your stride.

towards redcliff point

'Burning Cliff', a National Trust sign announces, for these slopes slumping to Ringstead Bay contain Kimmeridge's weird oil based shales. In 1826 locals were alarmed by lively flames and sulphurous smoke rising from the ground and it went on for three years. The oil shale had spontaneously combusted. This happened briefly in 1974, when temperatures of 350C were recorded at the surface. Destroyed rock was also found that would have needed a fire of 550C. No barefoot babes here.

Keep your boots tight too if you decide to take the steep and narrow Smugglers Path down White Nothe. This path was used in a dramatic chase in 'Moonfleet', John Meade Falkner's 1898 novel. Before or after, but not when tackling this boot-wide way, test the unnoticed role of your eyes in keeping you safe with every twist of the terrain. Before you do, on safe ground try balancing on one foot, then close your eyes and see what happens.

If choosing the more conventional approach, you'll pass ground covered in a stunning array of wild herbs and flowers. By the beach you'll also pass the first of ten caravan parks bang alongside this walk, though this one is very small. Imagine such fresh-air havens after busy city streets. Imagine a lazy week in surroundings which are even awesome to those who are used to them. In some of the larger sites, if it's the season you'll be able to refresh yourself at cafes or do a skip around many a sandcastle. Incongruous as such sites might seem, even though the larger ones raise questions about planning processes, the many holiday parks bring in revenue and provide local employment as tourist-cash spreads into the near by community, as does yours.

If you love magical little watery worlds briefly
isolated before being flushed by the rising
tide, the rock pools along the beach
contain sea anemones, crabs and who
knows what. With rocks from the
Kimmeridge, Purbeck and Portland beds,
you might find a variety of fossils, there
are also the famed fossilised coral beds
created when this area was as warm as
the Red Sea. Furthermore, a loo awaits
you as does a seasonal kiosk-shop. Walking
the clifftop west of this wee hamlet, a real
treat appears if the water happens to be calm.
Looking down, you'll see beautiful wavy patterns created by
bands of limestone splaying out from the cliffs. This hard stone
laid beneath what you are walking on twists like laminae of
plywood. It's the "Alpine Orogeny!"

The surprise of something new such as these creative swirls,
generates rapture. Apes feel this when suddenly coming across
a waterfall, they dance, they squeal with delight. Many of us
have rarely felt wonder since we left the encouraging
atmosphere of primary school and donned the 'cool' mindsets of
adolescence. We assume such things are fixed, but not at
all. Like these hard rocks, mindsets are malleable,
even dissolvable, all it takes is the desire to shift
and create others we prefer.

65 mya

In the 1790's, Osmington Mill was a lost wooded valley which had an inn that traded with the French smuggler Pierre Latour. Pierre would arrive to anchor off shore from the pub with contraband. Several government cutters from Weymouth tried to catch the rapid little L'Hirondelle and its reputed captain with a price on his head. On one occasion, being offered gin instead of his habitual brandy, Latour realised the publican, who was silently nodding towards the fireplace, was indicating that a customs official was hiding, hoping to catch him. Claiming to be cold, Latour demanded a fire was lit and the poor officer fell from the chimney spluttering and coughing as everyone laughed. Latour, who I'm sure could be cruel, magnanimously offered the wretch a brandy and let the humiliated fellow walk away unharmed but smothered in soot. Upon retiring from his trade, Latour married the landlord's daughter and spirited her off to France.

The eastern cliffs display a selection of fossils and there's a fault at Bran Point and a reef known as Bran Ledge. The foreshore is littered with fossil clams from a shallow Mediterranean sea, so with dinosaurs living on the nearby land and huge ammonites floating about in the sea, it's quite the place for a picnic.

Even more of a treat are the 'doggers', um, no, I'm not being rude. Eastwards along the beach at Bencliff are rounded boulders which some have compared to burger-buns, hinting that there once might have been giants, for these can be a metre across. These unusual features were formed individually within sandstone below the sea bed when calcium carbonate collected around decaying organic material over hundreds of thousands of years. These big dogger boulders often fall free from the softer sandstone cliff to embellish the beach.

The pub here is the only sustenance for some miles, so ensure you have sufficient food and water. In London's National Gallery hangs a Constable looking out across Weymouth Bay, painted in this inn when the artist was on honeymoon; one hopes he didn't spend all his time with his brushes. Not long after Osmington Mills, the softer terrain's slumping facade forces the path inland atop a wooded landslip which harbours a rare enclave whose creatures must be happy we humans must avoid this tangled environment. If you love fossils, the beach below Redcliff Point occasionally gives up fist-sized ammonites, but tightly tie those sturdy boots.

With this expansive view across the majesty of Weymouth Bay and Portland island, we leave the pristine chalk, confusion of limestones, messy hardened clays and enter a period when strata formed in a swampy, saline environment.

Move along with the wind tufting your hair, stroking your skin. Sink into your physical form, wallowing in the simple sensation of being alive. Appreciating what we are without fuss is a wholesome experience that gives rise to an instinctual awareness whose roots are deep in our ancient lineage.

Thank goodness Kevani, the Weymouth Bay beauty who lived here 150 millions years ago is no longer around as he might take off your toes before they tingle. Pliosaur Kevani, pieced together over ten years by Kevan Sheehan of Osmington, emerged from the Kimmeridge cliffs on Osmington beach. Kevani's crocy-jaws would snap you up without thought. Did dinosaurs think? Certainly; animals have foresight and act upon it, they also have 'attitude' and they can be swayed, and that seems to equal to thinking.

'Kevani, the local monster....
more on pliosaurs later

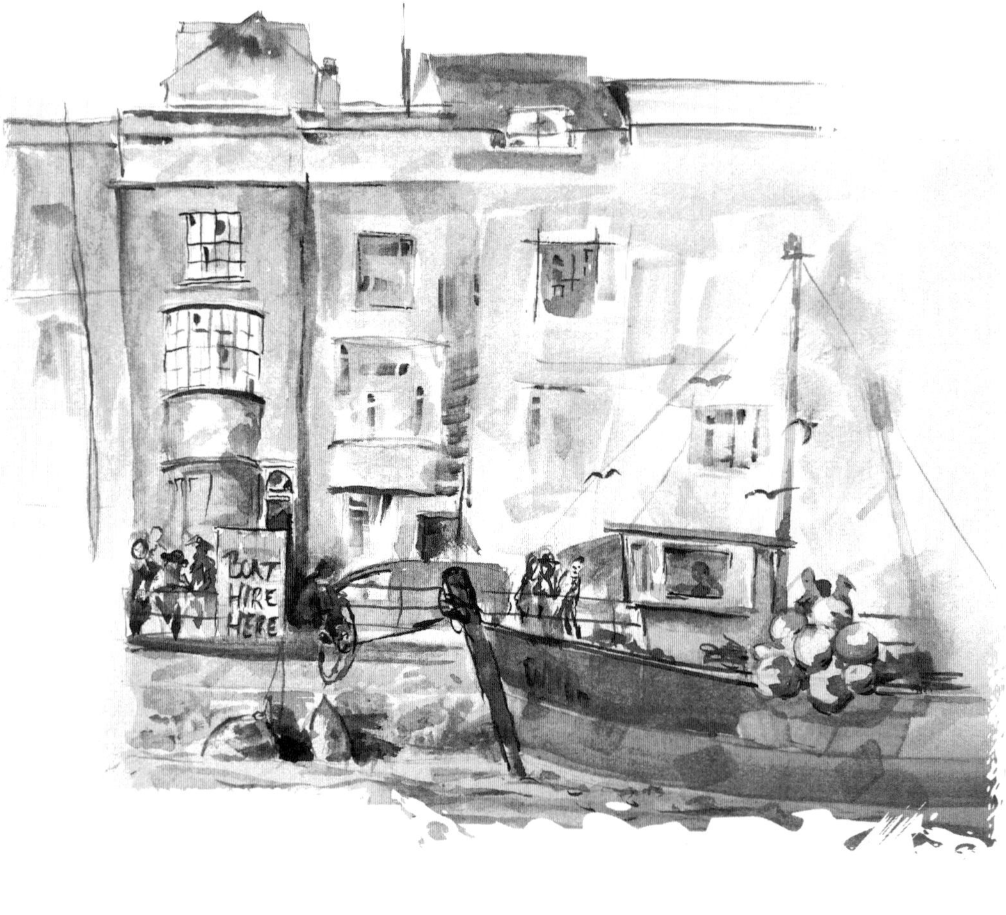
BOAT HIRE HERE

weymouth bay

The inland path as you dip into Weymouth Bay passes a caravan park. However, overlooking the private cliff tops stands The Riviera Hotel, a fine example of pre-War modernist architecture which has been listed as a classic. Completed in 1937, the 100 bedroom structure bankrupted the builder. As the next owner took possession, war began and the elegant rooms filled with children fleeing a London suffering bomb shattering terror. It must have been paradise for those frightened children. One wonders how many were aware that, as Historic England once put it: "The Riviera epitomises the austere approach of the pre-war modernists." Perhaps it was the arching colonnade effect that inspired a Saudi businessman to buy this well situated hotel, though it might simply have been an investment. Neglected in the years since, it fell into serious decline, despite a precursory renovation in 2012.

The beach yawning out before you is the largest since Studland and if it is a warm day, wiggle those hardworking toes in Bowleaze Bay's glowing sands and its scattering of shells. If a cold day, sensually relishing your booted feet sinking into a softer surface than a well trodden path will tease your mind towards the zone. Should the weather be favourable, you'll hopefully have your costume packed, for the sun warmed waters which cover this shallow expanse of sand are amongst the warmest on England's southern coast.

The bay is a delta created by several small rivers depositing sand and mud over time and in places it is quite swampy, which makes for the perfect nature haven. Should you have the time to linger, reed-beds, wet grassland and salt-marshes provide a species rich environment. If you love the stream of swimming water voles or the otter's brash splash, Weymouth's interlinked nature reserves are stimulating places to watch them scurry about beneath resident and migrating bird populations. In early spring you might be lucky to be entertained by marsh harriers sky-dancing.

Evolution is amazing. Take the dipper. Its small wings enable it to swim, it also has extra haemoglobin to absorb more oxygen and it's nostrils have underwater valves!

This easy bay is protected from NE and SW storms and so settlements began to form along the River Wey. Over the millennia the river had carried silt from the interior and deposited it as a spit that now curls from its mouth, just where the splendid beach ends. Since before Roman times, Weymouth's bay attracted sailors, Roman traders left their craft in the bay's natural harbour or tethered them to the banks of the river before heading inland to their new town, Dorchester. They had quickly taken the string of local hill-forts such as Flower's Barrow, Maiden Castle, Abbotsbury and distant Eggardon Hill which looms above Bridport.

In 1348, the Black Death first came to England through Weymouth via a ship from Venice. The disease trimmed off a third of the country's population. Some places lost 90% of their inhabitants, London rapidly shrank from 100,000 people to 20,000. This imbalanced the feudal system, as less labour forced the land owners and the rich to pay more; in a dark sense, Weymouth instigated the movement towards egalitarianism.

Weymouth was originally two settlements, each with their own harbour on either bank of the River Wey but they quarrelled so much over the centuries that, in 1571, Queen Elizabeth enjoined them to end their bitter hostilities. Seven years of Civil War from 1642, ruined much of the town, which took a long time to revive. Thank goodness for potty old King George III who visited in 1789 whilst France buckled under revolution.

'Taking Sea Water!' was popular and preparing himself for a cure for his dottiness, the king and his large entourage spent weeks going to the theatre, strolling along the promenade and enjoying the town which he came to love. One imagines the King didn't enjoy the recommended pills of crushed crab's eyes, burnt sponge, viper's flesh, snails, tar, cuttle-fish bones and dried wood-lice downed with a slug of sea water.

On the chosen day, shops displayed banners proclaiming 'God Save the King!' His freshly painted bathing machine was wheeled out to cheers from the crowds ashore as well as those bobbing in the surrounding boats. As he edged down the steps: "The 'dippers' seized him and firmly dunked him under the waves as music struck 'God Save Great George our King' and Weymouth resounded with cheers," one diarist noted.

Good old George was most likely 'dipped' by great Martha Gunn, "A brawny old Queen of the Brighton briny who lived to the ripe age of 75, mercilessly plunging squealing young ladies, yelling children and shivering men of all ages into the English Channel."

Weymouth became one of George's favourite places to take the waters and he and his hangers-on created a boom, giving the town many fine buildings - in the area there are roughly 1,400 listed buildings. Protecting old buildings is not always popular, particularly amongst developers. However, scientific monitoring shows people walk quickly through bland modern structures, they are inattentive, edgy, more cortisone floods their blood, over time this chemical induces negative metabolic changes which influences our health. In contrast, along old streets people move more slowly, they look around absorbing detail and beauty, they smile more.

Sadly, quaint seaside towns attract wealthier incomers and rising house prices shove locals out. The influx increases the spurt of new buildings - Weymouth's urban scape has more than quadrupled in recent years. Across the expanse of England this is alarming, considering our population has increased only by 18%. Construction worldwide emits 11% of CO_2, six times that emitted by airplanes. As old property is renovated or pulled down, waste from the industry amounts to 65% of Britain's refuse volume.

Weymouth beach boasts two of England's last three Punch&Judy shows, I once wrote about the third at Llandudno. Arriving three years after England emerged from the bleak years of Cromwell's Taliban-like rule (he closed all theatres), Punch's official UK birthday is 1662. This light-hearted theatre, a variation of the Lord of Misrule, derives from an Italian tradition of street theatre called Pulcinella.

The puppeteers' task is to make children giggle and to tease their parents with political satire. The longevity of these open-air shows is threatened by the number of tourists aggressively refusing to contribute the tiny fee. Though passionate about their art, the two disheartened local families must pay rent, taxes and insurance as they eek out their meagre living.

Centuries ago, the safe bay attracted a naval presence and during WW1 it was a torpedo base; WW2 saw the town and port being bombed by the Nazis. Nearly 250,000 American personnel passed through the town as they prepared for D-Day, the world's greatest ever invasion. You wonder what the birds in the important wetlands thought of all that military activity. Now in private hands, the port itself handles a variety of shipping activities, from cruise ships to refugee barges and cargo boats.

Looking out across the expanse of calm waters, you realise why Weymouth Bay was chosen as the main water sports venue during the 2012 Olympics. What a fine stretch upon which to chase the wind. Today it is thrilling to watch world class sporty types testing their skills against one another.

The Covid pandemic filled the Bay with large cruise and cargo ships, reminding folk of the days when our ports were crammed with boats of all shapes and sizes. However, gazing at the ostentatious cruise liners sheltering here stirred up questions about the impact of our excesses. The CO_2 cost of constructing those floating blocks of luxury, to say nothing of their daily over-consumption, add on their future decommissioning, the pollutants ....

The walk south along the old railway line which once carried stone from Portland to Weymouth and beyond, offers views across the harbour. Stepping sideways you could inspect two ancient castles which prove the importance of this once swampy little spot. This old causeway's end has been swept away by waters pouring back and forth from an inland slick called the Fleet which lies between the land and the pebble bank of Chesil Beach.

The architecture of our improved roads, the concrete bridges, they hold us back from reality - as we fly along, everywhere can look the same bar the odd hill or river. Detached, we drift along, hardly noticing when the tide rises or falls. Lean over these concrete balustrades, look without thought at the swirling water, imagine crossing this without any bridge. If a storm is currently swirling the entrance to the Fleet lagoon, be awed that when winds bombed the hills this was once a dangerous passageway. Step from your human bubble, watch trepidation stir within, mentally ride its swell and let the wind rasp your eyelashes, the rain chill your finger tips. Sense the animal inside rise and feel vitally alive. Linger here, for this is the cusp where life happens.

stormy Portland Bill and a yacht testing Portland Race

portland

Portland, a door-wedge of strata which Thomas Hardy called 'the Gibraltar of Wessex". Tethered to the mainland by a slither of pebbles, an almost treeless and windswept rock 4.5 miles long by a max width of 2. Tilted from an elevation of 151m to just 3m above sea level, Portland was formed in a Caribbean environment with reefs and lush warm lagoons when the tourists had very long necks and spoke dinosorous 150 million years ago.

Upon arriving at the summit of this strange island, it is worth peering in to the grounds of a previous hotel called 'Heights' atop Tophill, (exactly), where stands a large fossil tree against which the odd dino might well have scratched her back. Giant ammonites up to a metre across swam about here, these, trees and other fossilised creatures can be found in Portland's limestone quarries.

Standing upon the island's dramatic northern edge, sensing the enormity of the timespan before you, the entirety of human history becomes but a dot. This is suitably humbling. We may be proud that our specific civilisation spans 300, 1,000 or at best 9,000 years, but it was only a mere 2 million years ago that we first used fire. Yet the insects sneaking past our feet existed when dinosaurs snored the night away, many were so well formed that they have continued in the exact shape they had long before this rocky bulk was lifted from the seabed.

150 mya

We the newbies, need to protect the dwindling number of minute creatures and large! Our governments and business are too bound up in consumerism's Gordian knot to untangle it for us. They need our money, ergo we have power, so let's untie that tangle.

Britain's 'des-res' spots began to feel a little over crowded as various clans and tribes immigrated across from Europe. One group knew that Portland was a place to live without fear and locals have long claimed that they have tinges of Phoenician blood. That is a possibility, the bay's safe anchorage has long attracted seafarers. Portlanders were, until quite recently, strongly independent and wouldn't allow non-islanders to buy property on their bleak, quarry-dented island. They were proud to regard themselves as an insular breed, different from 'Kimberlins', as they called us mainlanders. Could this explain why they are apparently afraid to say 'the R word' (as in the Forest of Dean, they won't mention the word bear). They can call them bunnies or long eared mutton, never rabbits, oops, which aren't the 'Portland mutton' found on Dorset menus - a rare breed of recently revived hardy black-faced sheep.

In 789, a little before Vikings turned Normandy into their power base, England's first Viking landing occurred on this isle. At about this time, the Saxons gave the islanders a kind of independence from Dorset. The Portland Manor power and rent collecting system existed until 1905, when Parliament in London jealously withdrew the privilege. During Saxon times, the term 'manor' meant the smallest administrative unit after 'hundreds' and the larger 'shires'. Saxon England divided society into: 'thanes', the upper-crust who hunted and feasted; beneath them the 'churls' either owned their homes or paid rent through part-time labour to thanes. Many churls began to lose their freedom and soon became 'thralls', really slaves for the thanes, and their lives were tough.

Most Saxons lived in single-roomed thatched wooden huts with their animals behind a dividing screen, this helped heat their rudimentary homes in winter. In their halls lit by rushes steeped in animal fat, thanes slept on beds whilst their slaves lay on the earthen floor. The Saxons had outside toilets, secreted within wattle walls, they crouched on wooden seats with the requisite hole.

In Saxon times England was a stable, rich and well governed country. The entire country had a population of about one million living in villages boasting fewer than 100 inhabitants. Secreted within the abundant forest cover, they needed few things from outside and they traded their excess for salt or iron. Roughly 10% of the population lived in towns; no wonder the Normans invaded.

Up on Tophill there is evidence of strip farming where oxen pulled ploughs to sow rye, barley and wheat. As well as parsnips, carrots and peas, people grew soft fruit beneath apple trees. The neighbouring strip lay fallow for a year, enriched by the manure of the owner's handful of goats, pigs, cattle and sheep which grazed common land. What an example for today, but not here where the land has been ravaged by quarrying. Portland is also over crowded, which is an unspoken problem, in 50 years world population has multiplied four times. But do I want to lay down my life so that you can better survive? Difficult....

Beware, upon Portland, there's the Underhill and Tophill lot, the former once fished and their offspring still live mostly on the northern slopes, whilst the top crowd farmed and quarried. Up on Tophill in 1541, King Henry of the many wives, built the imposing Portland Castle. He was concerned about the wrath of European countries who despised his splitting away from the Catholic Church so that he could marry as he pleased.

Over time, Portland's remoteness led to a maximum security prison being placed high up here in Henry's castle and the views from its cells would be hard to beat. Today, it even has a popular cafe called Jailhouse Cafe.

A lovely old map from 1710 shows the only quarry was in the north east, above the King's Pier. From here stone went to rebuild London after fire destroyed the mostly wooden city in 1666. We must thank Sir Christopher Wren, who came from Weymouth, for using Portland stone on the plethora of Wren churches and buildings. This white limestone adorns such buildings as St Paul's Cathedral, Buckingham Palace as well as the UN building in New York. Not only is Portland a beautiful stone, it is durable yet easy to work. Such pure limestone occurs when less mud and dirt are laid down as calcium settles on shallow sea beds.

Portland's horizontal strata has regular vertical joints which match the island's outline, this enables the limestone to be extracted in conveniently sized blocks. The poor prisoners had to quarry the hard stone and haul it down to the bay and toss it into the sea to create a protective harbour. The first mention of a breakwater was in 1749; come 1847, the prisoners must have been delighted to use an inclined railway to help extend the breakwater. Holidaying Victorians must have been bored, for Portland attracted tourists who came to watch the prisoners work.... Queen Victoria's Prince Albert witnessed this over 23 years and he finally laid a stone commemorating the creation of the world's largest man-made harbour in 1872. The breakwater was again extended between 1896 and 1905 and even now it is the world's 4th largest, with over 2.8 miles of breakwater.

Talking of tourism, Portland has witnessed an increase in second homes as well as outsiders buying houses for holiday rentals. This means many locals can no longer afford to live, or even rent in their homeland. Once a seaside disease, this trend has spread inland across SW England, forcing those from the area, whose wages are generally lower than the British average, to move away to less desirable locations. Workers often abide in caravans hidden from view so that they can be near to where they earn money. These people man our essential services, some are in seasonal employment such as tourism, for the usual rural activities like agricultural endeavours and cottage industries have diminished.

Walking past the popular cove of Church Ope, the ancient sea-access to this isle, you will note that old tarred fishermen's huts are being replaced by modern beach huts. Back inland between the Tophill villages of Easton and Weston, two stout windmill towers which pre-date 1608, overlook an open quarry which seems about to swallow one of them, but don't get the wind in your sails, they are bare of anything but their stone walls. These structures resemble those of Mediterranean windmills, showing the extent of trading connections these islanders have had.

That this thin lump of rock sticks out from the curve of Lyme Bay means that the English Channel's infamous tidal rushes are made more powerful here. Furthermore, at its snout, Portland Bill's hard rock continues south just beneath the sea's surface, helping to create the famed swirls of the Portland Race.

Making this area even more menacing are the twin sandbanks of Portland Banks and the Shambles to the island's east. Three lighthouses were constructed on the island and even today approaching ships are cautious, for 400 shipwrecks surround the isle. The worst wreck was in 1805, when the Earl of Abergavenny, a merchant ship off to China, struck the extremely shallow Shambles in a storm. 260 people drowned, including the skipper, who was the poet William Wordsworth's brother and it is claimed the news affected the quality of his poetry. The ship still lies beneath the waves. There is even a church called Avalanche, built after a clipper of that name struck a ship called Forest, with a heavy loss of life in 1877.

In 1949, before they had properly prepared their small yacht for sea, a couple called Frank and Ann set sail in a rush to avoid repossession. They floundered in Portland's rough seas and only Ann Davidson survived to scale the cliffs. She went on to become the first woman to sail alone across the Atlantic.

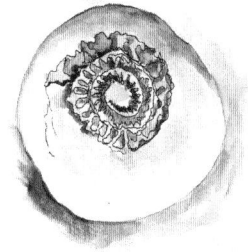

Water seeps through the massive limestone to rest on the Kimmeridge clays below, this lubricates slips which tumble hefty blocks, so be careful stepping on these clifftops. Returning to the island's north, peering over Chesil Bank's faint chain of pebbles, if you rub out the bridge you certainly get the impression that they hold Portland to the mainland. In common with Gibraltar, Portland is a tombolo. For those who don't gamble, this is Chesil Beach's defining geomorphological glory - a tombolo is a spit of pebbles or sand which veers from the mainland and attaches itself to an island. Mont St Michel across the waters in Normandy is another example.

Even on a normal day, water rushes in and out between the expanse of Weymouth Bay and the watery narrows of The Fleet, generating crazy currents. Until a wooden bridge was built in 1839, folk used to traverse on small boats held straight by hemp ropes anchored to each shore. In 1865, to carry Portland's glistening building stone upcountry, the (long gone) railway line you recently walked along, crossed the Fleet's snout upon a wooden edifice which rested on stone pillars.

Thankfully this crossing was replaced by a more solid steel one in 1896. Fast forward 90 years. A study of the extreme storms which regularly flood this corner of the coast suggested a complex system of sea banks and drainage holes with an underground tunnel. Some mocked this as the 'monsoon ditch", but storm waters now easily flow out from the Bay and into the sea without entering The Fleet or endangering Portland's old fishing settlement of Fortuneswell. Today's winter storms cause little damage in comparison to the havoc wreaked by earlier gales. Due to those inventive engineers, the severe unpredictability of climate change ought to be less of a worry.

Step lightly across this man-made beginning of the tombolo and relish the wonder of being able to stand upright. As our weight shifts from side to side with each step, multiple muscles and tendons adjust our posture. Each tiny dip, the tilt of the land, the tenderness of the terrain has us instinctually reacting. Shifting attention to physical sensations, we are entranced by the body's marvels, gradually our sense of self realigns. The gripping stream of thought playing out in the theatre of our many selves continues, but the conflict between our mind's desires and the brain's responses eases. A sense of completeness starts to emerge.

Chesil Bar reaching out from Portland and Weymouth

around chesil beach

If you were to leave this isle by swimming westwards from Fortuneswell's curved beach, Venezuela would be the next land your frozen fingers would strike. From the Caribbean, roughly every 250 years, hurricanes spin across 4,350 miles of sea to crash enormous waves upon these pebbles at your feet. Big storms are now much more frequent.

Dramatic as a widely reported storm of 2016 might well have been, it was a comparative toddler and its effects were greatly lessened by those heroic engineers of the 1980's. Take the Great Gale of November 1824. The waves in this near-tsunami were 3-4 m high - imagine a water-wall as high as a row of cottages speeding towards you. A naval captain said it resembled a tropical hurricane. The sea howled, the wind screeched, the storm terrified locals used to fierce south-westerlies. Boats were tossed inland, in Weymouth and local villages falling chimneys crushed folk in their homes. The Western Flying Post termed it, "A tempest teeming with... frightful terrors...." 50 people died a few paces from where you are about to begin your swim to South America.

Richard Best, the ferryman to Portland, drowned as he tried to rescue a stranded horse caught in the outflow of the Fleet. To have known such a gallant man.... Waves destroyed eighty houses. "Many remained trapped under the ruins of their former homes, as others were dangerously wounded in their courageous endeavours to rescue friends and relatives from death," from the diary of a resident at the time.

Wild 'sea-horses' rushed up and over Chesil Beach's protective barrier of pebbles. That is quite something as the height of this gigantic stone pile can rise to between 15-18 metres above sea level. At the village of Fleet itself, those fierce marine stallions sped almost a mile from the sea and up the little stream to demolish a couple of cottages. The ancient church which stood 11m above sea-level was destroyed and this being a smuggler's haven, contraband hidden within a family vault was lost, to say nothing of the bones. This storm devastated the harbour at West Bay 20 miles further west and all along the coast bodies were washed up for days on end.

Back at those heroic man-made sea defences lies Dorset Wildlife Trust's attractive building and a visit now will reward you later as you move along the Fleet path. DWT is one of 46 which knit together to do excellent work across the UK. Here they have a boat which provides an enchanting, informative guide to life in and around The Fleet lagoon.

The Coastal Path skirts the inner shore of this dreamlike lagoon and upon leaving the urban sprawl and a caravan site, you'll soon come across Moonfleet Manor. Now a hotel, the manor was the inspiration for the novel 'Moonfleet'.

For two miles, between beach and farmed fields, between the turbulent sea and the rising land, the Fleet's saline calmness has encouraged reeds to thrive. This has created a magical zone for wildlife to flourish. Slow your step, try to locate the birds singing, can you spot any amphibians? Be wary of stamping on your ancient, ancient forebears and the insects who love this haven.

Our own ancestors understood their environment, it made them alert, alive. I grew up alongside people with a detailed

black veined butterfly

knowledge of the many inter-connected systems surrounding them. Quietly ecological, practical, agrarian, deeply present, their tales intertwined with the surrounding complexity and spoke of their minute role in it all. They didn't kill predators seeking their cattle but faced the hungry leopard or lion until it retreated. Those trustworthy people who begat Kenya's long-distant Olympic runners were like no others I have met since.

Dorset Wildlife Trust say the Fleet attracts dunlin, oyster catchers, little egret and ringed plover as well as hundreds of Brent geese and other migrating or over-wintering wildfowl. In spring a rare colony of little terns breed on the beach. There are hares, rare crickets and snails living and multiplying on this special expanse of shingle. In May the stoney bar becomes a wave of pink sea thrift sprinkled with sea campion, scarlet pimpernel, kidney vetch, yellow horn poppy and other coastal specialists. No wonder this is part of a Marine Protected Area.

We don't always realise it, but we humans dig and bounce and stride upon a refined web of interconnected, pulsating eco systems. Each attuned to its neighbour, each overlapping and interacting, each filled with intelligent creatures finely tuned to exploit their own delicately balanced niche.

Blinded by squalls, ancient fishermen forced to land on this enormously long bar would bend down, scoop up a handful of pebbles. By their size they'd work out where they were - big at Portland, pea-sized approaching Burton Bradstock.

Fleet fishermen have traditionally used two specific rowing boats - the lerret which is pointed at both ends so that it can be rowed in either direction by four people. The other, the Fleet Trow, is flat bottomed so that after use in the waves, it can be hauled to safety up the pebble bank.

Only fools attempt to walk Chesil's 18 miles of pebbles, even a 200m stomp is arduous. Where did all these stones come from? Storms release bed rock from the cliffs reaching out to the blue beyond, heavy waves pound the fallen chunks to bits and over the thousands of centuries they are tumbled, rounded and brought here. Others have a history reaching back hundreds of millions of years.

Pebbles are carried along a beach by waves tossing them in and then pulling them out at an angle, the next wave does the same, creating a Z Z Z movement. To confuse the issue, there's two long-shore drift currents, a weaker one from Portland heading west, a stronger Atlantic one shifting things eastwards. But there's something odd near the Weymouth end. 2% of pebbles are from Budleigh Salterton, which is 45 wave-miles away! How, one must ask? Well, imagine frisbees in the water - the bigger surface area creates a lift advantage…. but it is perplexing and experts still argue over this pebble problem, hopefully without tossing them at each other.

non specific boats on a choppy morning

Chasing a stream which ends by a weeping spring, the rising path swings inland through patchy woods and fields and the Fleet's natural environment gives way to intensely farmed slopes. Fortunes are spent killing off insects and weeds with chemicals. Low intensity farming requires less investment, hence less repayments, and provides roughly the same raw income in the pocket, though less productivity. Let the insects help, allowing hedgerows to grow wider, creating safe eco-strips along which little beasts spread in all directions to revive lost habitats. Ladybirds and others eat the aphids, a harmony gradually returns which grants both the farmer and a myriad of species a healthy coexistence.

Trying these laudable aims in an attempt to feed us, needs careful thought; without government help it has to be a brave farmer to make this shift. Yet a growing number of such folk are emerging, encouraged by the discerning consumer. That is our power, if we buy local, persuade all our friends to, the swell will, if we are all persistent, change the economics. Unintentionally, over three hundred years we've slipped into an efficiency/profit driven system where vast companies control us like slaves... to their gain.

The Coastal Path rises 80 metres and as it levels, 500m onwards you'll be wowed by Abbotsbury village's splay of thatched stone cottages, there's shops and a pub too. In 1752 The London Journal wrote: "All the people of Abbotsbury, including the vicar, are thieves, smugglers and plunderers of wrecks." Today houses cost more than the average plunderer might afford, again the problem locals face from second homes and in-migration from one of the world's wealthiest zones - London and her billowing skirt.

The high ridge above has over 22 ancient tumuli and two ridge-top forts, showing that people have liked living hereabouts for over 5,000 years. No wonder. Protected from cold north winds by the imposing Ridgeway, a feature thrown up in one of the Alpine quakes 50 million years ago, the village has its own micro-climate.

The heart skipping view over Chesil Beach, east to Portland, west across Lyme Bay and on to the distant trace of Start Point 56 miles away, the stitching of land to sea and sky! You sense why they placed St Catherine's chapel up here in the 1300's, a barrel vaulted beauty to inspire monks. The enormity shakes the ego, prompting a desire for the comforting security of a universal plan which will grant purpose. The wishing holes drew women desperate for husbands, so be careful what you ask for at this elevated point.

a tern

It is claimed that Britain's first church stood here, a wooden edifice which saw invading Saxons harbour their longboats in the Fleet in about 410. This could be so. In 304, a Christian later to be called St Alban, was executed in a place near London which gained his name. In 313 Emperor Constantine granted Christians freedom of worship, encouraging the faith to spread throughout the Roman Empire. A year later three British bishops attended a church council in Arles in southern France, they had Roman names - Eborius bishop of York, Restitutus bishop of London and Adelius bishop of Gwent.

During breaks from recording, the view must also have touched George, Ringo and Paul when they first attempted, but failed to make a decent record of John's "Now and then" in the 1990's. However, this hallowed ridge above the sweep of Chesil Beach, must have helped the remaining Beatles record John's "Free as a Bird" and "Real Love".

Almost 600 hundred years after the Saxons arrived, King Canute whom the waves loved to wet, gave his bodyguard, Orc, the parish of Abbotsbury. The strongman built an abbey, from which the Swannery downhill derives, for those large birds fed the Benedictine monks. This sanctuary is another rewarding detour, particularly if you prefer not to eat swans. Our Kings and Queens have the right over all swans. Ensuring this is the Royal Swan Marker, a man who looks as if he ought to be in a circus, with a pillar box red coat, black trousers and a swan feather jauntily decorating a military hat.

The elegance of floating swans, nesting swans, the delight of cygnets, the joy of their huge wings beating water, followed by the air squeaking between their flying feathers. Flap this graceful video through your mind's eye, glide over emotional turmoil. Learning to soar from internal swamps is a useful skill, mood is triggered by thought-chains and such positive mental pictures ignite brighter mindsets....

The stark, almost haunting aura felt as you stand alone on Chesil's mounded extent of rounded stones inspired Ian McEwan to set a novel here. A decade later, 'On Chesil Beach' became an emotive film that captures a newly married man's inept ability to relate. Here's a wee taster: "He could have called out to Florence … and she would have turned back."

You could refresh your tired legs at West Bexington, a thin settlement rising from the pebbles to the ridge so far above. Should your pockets be over full, you might wish to spend a small fortune on one of the beach huts, some of the older ones are as spacious as a one bedroomed London flat. Evacuate though when wild storms speed this way and throw truck-loads of pebbles at you.

The hollow clatter of waves rushing through steeply piled pebbles soon gives way to the swish of bubbles slushing up a low incline of sand. The booming as the beach steepens. The rustle as the seas rolls across the shallows. An oceanic symphony with uplifting melodies which teases the senses, untangles the emotions.

Sparing an hour or two to stride a short way up the road from near where the path from Abbotsbury hits Chesil Beach is well worth the effort. You reach a valley hidden in the rumpled up clays. It has a warm micro-climate stuffed with extraordinary plants. This haven began its life in 1765 as a walled vegetable garden to feed Stephen Strangeways, the first Earl of Ilchester. Since the wars against Napoleon, these Subtropical Gardens are filled with exotic life. You will come across the Strangeways again, so do remember the name.

It is heartening that such lush spots exist and many of our estates harbour copses and forests. We are lucky to have the Woodland Trust which *"plants, protects and conserves trees and woods"* across the country and is manned by 500,000 volunteers. They encourage these refuges to be as natural as possible in the knowledge that a tree shelters multiple species which have evolved together with over tens of millions of years, creating a complex, interdependent ecosystem. Oaks, for example, first came into being about 56 million years ago; wrote a person whose forebear existed much less than one million years ago; humility or what.... Deadwood is left to rot for it invites fungi, which attract specific flies and other insects that feed other creatures and the decay sinks minerals and nutrients into the soil. Thank goodness the Woodland Trust owns over 1,000 such sanctuaries.

an old oak

burton bradstock

If wave-washed toes tickles your fancy, you'll find, as you walk the washy inflow that you'll have to dip beneath fishermen's lines. These folk come from miles to Hive beach and they toss their hooks into the rolling waves and many take their catch back home. It's more a meditation than a sport, they say, but they do admit that there's fishing for summer mackerel, autumn bass and winter cod, though stocks are dwindling. Fish cooked minutes after being caught on a pan over wood is as good as it gets, but use driftwood with care. When burnt, its salts transmute into sodium and chloride which release carcinogenic particles. Some fools bury the hot detritus, which scorches passing toes. Why! The sea's wetness is strides away.

If you're flush, at Hive beach the National Trust has allowed a seafood restaurant to flourish. There's also an ice cream business to tempt you... this ought to be called the Creamy Coast. Thankfully, a Coast Watch station manned by volunteers ensures ice cream doesn't end up in local cream teas, no, they too do the serious work previously outlined. Smuggling as such began when the Saxon King Ethelred the Unready (966-1016) taxed wine arriving near London. In 1275, King Edward 1 taxed outgoing English wool which was in great demand abroad and by the 1300's the first revenue cruisers patrolled the ports and estuaries (leaving the rest of the coast unguarded). Customs men were poorly paid and corruption was widespread, however, William Lowe was incorruptible and in 1452 he seized a Dutch ship filled with untaxed goods from Bridport, Sherborne and Charminster.

However, it wasn't always straightforward. In 1719, quantities of brandy and salt from a wreck were "carried off by great numbers of country people" in full view of Customs staff. One man cunningly paid duty on dried tobacco which he then hydrated to increase its weight before selling it, gaining 40% extra tax free. In 1720, out from Burton Bradstock beach fishermen discovered brandy and wine barrels sunken with "ropes moored to stones", some of which they "naturally took."

Another time, casks belonging to the famed smuggler, 'the Colonel of Bridport', floated from their sunken mooring to shore and were impounded by Customs in Abbotsbury. Who said they were all rotten? Well, the load was taken (read stolen) by the Lord of the Manor, one Thomas Strangeways, whose offspring were to create those tropical gardens. Strangeways employed just about everyone in Abbotsbury and when the army were called in by Customs they faced "a great mob" but eventually reclaimed the goods. Strangeways pleaded that the casks were salvaged from a wreck and complained to the Secretary at War, even persuading gentlemen friends to raise the matter in Parliament. To no avail.

Ghost stories might have been spread by local smugglers to keep straying minds inside at night. A headless dog supposedly haunts the dark road and a headless coachman drives four headless horses through Burton Bradstock at midnight. Headless or drunk and legless? Those smugglers of old might have done better digging for ancient treasures, for in Burton Bradstock, known to the Domesday Book of 1086 as Bridetona, Roman bowls were discovered when an old house was recently extended.

The soft sandy and clay hills disappear here by Hive beach where, 140 million years ago tremendous pressure from tectonic movement formed a grid of fault lines. Abruptly west of this blemish rise the golden cliffs of Bridport Sands (they're compact and hard). Protruding from these sudden and impressive cliffs, a small promontory with recesses and arches existed until successive storms dissolved this little bluff of golden sandstone. Such events wear rock to the pebbles you have passed for so long, which is fitting as East Cliff is the end, or if you wish, the start of Chesil Beach. In the cliff itself, storm spray has attractively sculptured the layers of soft and hard stone, there's even the odd little dogger similar to those at Osmington Mills.

These cliffs are fragile, huge chunks tumble off regularly, as the path atop them shows - it is constantly moved inland to avoid danger. Do read the warning panels.

Maybe you'd be happy to stay back on the beach stirring your inner artist by creating a design with pebbles … Or go for a drink or a meal with a stunning view at the hotel atop the cliff.

Weirdly, as I edit this page, a protest song plays on the radio. The singer who wrote it has a mansion near this spot. One of the advantages of consumerism is that you can chant against it and make yourself rich; having bought such records, I am part of this ecologically unbalancing process.

Not far inland lies the most perfect of manorial homes. Mapperton is famed for its alluring gardens which follow the tight little valley beneath the charmed Elizabethan manor. One of the country's biggest re-wilding projects is underway on this ancient estate where 450 acres have been set aside to put nature first. Two beavers are busy building a dam which is creating a complex, rich ecosystem that will attract many species. Exmoor ponies, cousins of New Forest ponies, which crop grass unevenly so allowing a host of insects to thrive, have also been introduced.

Mapperton is the Earl of Sandwich's home. Though sandwiches were named after one of his ancestor's, in the USA the family was prevented from using their name commercially. The 'sarnie' is the karma of gambling, which is what the sandwich Earl was doing when he ordered a slice of ham between two bits of bread. And that's the problem with excess. Bored aristocrats gambled whilst the poor slaved, starved and died in dreadful conditions. One hundred years ago, my paternal family's vast fortune thus fled… to another card holder. Today, when the disparity between the wealthy and the average person has never been greater, those in need gamble more than ever, perhaps hoping to improve their lives .

Gain is an integral part of nature, faster, bigger dinosaurs with sharper teeth gained dominance. Our little reptilian-type ancestors were good at gambling and thus survival, but remember, they handed us anxiety, an off-shot of the wager. If afflicted by anxiety it is handy to remember that our innate selves are affected by calm breathing and by feeling our bodies. Relaxing as we slowly let air out is soothing. This deeper self senses that it is safe, we feel calm, at peace.

west bay plus

Beware of 'the white lady' who wanders these clifftops, nor be tempted to sunbathe at the foot of the beautifully banded cliff from which she flies. Whatever the season, these enticing, bulbous ramparts discard rock laid down 180 million years ago. In a split second you'd merge with fossilised dinos. Seagulls nesting in the gnarled strata shoot skywards and one such blast took the white lady into the stormy night.

Puffing along the tops lets you see how the strata tips steeply northwards from this popular cliff top walk. Singing with the sighing sea so far below, step with the wind licking your legs. Such is life's fuel, these mad moments when you feel eternal.

As you dip into a sheltered vale, give a nod to the next holiday park filled with static caravans, a haven, a delight for those whose little abodes are 18 floors above busy city ring roads. Architects have a lot to answer for. You'll smile with the stream which heads back to Burton Bradstock.

From this holiday valley you rise to traipse past a golf course and down you go on this natural rollercoaster to strike West Bay. Few cliff faces are as alluring as this one. Golden early in the day, scarlet at sunset, sandy in the sun's full blast, layered with the fine sand of beaches long frozen, indented by bands of knobbly fossilised forms. A facade of a thousand mini waterfalls when it pours.

180 mya

On a warm evening, the bustle of life in West Bay engages the social sensibilities. From far and wide come bicycles, motor bikes, cars and even boots which have trod the coastal path. The lively food stalls cater to all tastes and many are keen to be as sustainable as possible, buying from the fishing boats which still come and go between the flotilla of private power boats, canoes and inflatable dinghies. If you are here in August, celebrate West Bay Day with boat races, seafood cook-offs, classic cars and live music.

This is the harbour that kept moving. Once a mile inland as a small landing area in Bridport, the river silted up and so goods had to be transported by cart from where ships docked beneath the cliffs 300m east of the present harbour. The river meandered and the harbour had to move west, only to be remoulded continuously as nature threatened the tiny port. Eventually the dock was stabilised with two long protective piers that hold back the ever shifting shingle.

A good thing too, as this was the vital exporter of the Bridport Dagger, or hangman's nose. Since before the 1200's, Bridport's busy industries produced rope, nets and sailcloth which flowed out to the wider world in the holds of ships. Huge quantities of hemp and flax were grown in villages as far away as Crewkerne, explaining why there are so many fine houses locally. Well, that and the local sheep's wool which was prized all over Europe.

Flax, meaning 'very useful' because it can be eaten and is a traditional medicine, makes canvas, cloth and paper and was in use in Switzerland 8,000 years ago. Hemp found in Iraq and Iran 10,000 years ago, makes rope, paper and quality cloth and is a biodegradable alternative to plastics.

This flourishing economy accounted for Bridport's many mills and warehouses as well as its wide streets where rope was 'walked' together. The town boasts Britain's oldest continuously trading family - Balson Butcher's who've been trading since 1515, their shop is beyond the western end of the main street. The huge Saturday and smaller Wednesday markets abound with stalls selling a variety of food, clothing, hardware, flowers, pictures, antiques and paintings, and they attract large crowds. The town has a superbly silly hat festival in September, a summer food fest, as well as a literary one too, not to mention the carnival and other lively events. Sitting in the Bucky Doo beneath the Town Hall, you often find yourself being entertained by live musical acts.

Today a stimulating arty set has made the town an attractive place to live, soaring house prices, yet again those whose families have lived for here centuries can't easily buy houses. All over this attractive area villages are sought after and mostly now inhabited by new arrivals with bigger pockets. This is one of the sadnesses of a free-market economy.

At low tide the walk west from West Bay saves you the trek up the steep cliff path. But beware, the incoming sea quickly swallows this strip of land beneath the clays and sands that slowly sink from the bulbous hills that terminate here. Sneak into these flopped folds of slumping slope with care, for faults within the clays may not be as solidly covered as they might seem.

eype & co

Pretty little Eype tucked back from her attractive beach's raging winter storms, established as a humble fisher-folks' settlement. The once little known beach grew in popularity over lockdown, but you can still find solitude as you search for tiny fossils shining with pyrites in the flopping dark grey clays, dastardly called the Black layers.

The National Trust owns the organically farmed land above, consequently there's a healthy diversity of birds, wildflowers, bees and butterflies and if it's spring, bluebells galore in the woods. The farmhouse is set well back in a fold of land quite a distance from Thorncombe Beacon. This beacon is one of a chain, lit when invaders threatened our shores or nowadays illuminated to celebrate national moments such as when King Charles III was crowned.

Start Point is 50 miles west, unseen Normandy 80 miles south is closer than Swansea, inland the eye travels across ancient hill-top forts which dominate bubbly land which Rupert Bear would have loved. This spot owes its drama to being capped by Bridport sands and by hard limestone, as well as a remnant of the chalks which stand so proudly above the seas further east.

This vantage is at infinity's edge, beneath the vastness of the sky, above the endless sea. Lingering between our own insignificance and life's abundant vitality, we are enriched.

Downwards you trudge past a little feature you might easily miss which is called Doghouse. Fittingly, a dog walker recently discovered this pre-farming settlement used by hunter-gatherers of the Mesolithic Age 10,000 years ago, a tad before we invented tinned dog food. At that time this spot was a mile inland and today it is being threatened by the erosion of the cliffs below, showing how the environment has changed. "To find ancient pottery decorated with fingernail impressions and touch them with one's own hand, that's real contact with the past!" said Martin Papworth of the National Trust in 2009. Excavations had uncovered a stone hearth, a fire pit, as well as pot shards from the Bronze Age (2500 to 1000 BC), and items dating back to those hunter-gatherers.

It was fire and the ability to sew hides into protective clothing which enabled our ancestors to exist in what was then a harsh, arctic zone. The equally amazing invention of pottery enabled them to better control what they cooked, multiplying the energy food provided. They had moved with the animals they hunted, much as modern tribes still do in the Artic Circle and parts of Africa.

The path drops to one of the walk's few seaside pubs at Seatown, which is no town. If you need a swim, be aware that the shore often dips away steeply and that there are rip currents. If ever you are tugged out, try ferry-gliding, it once saved my wife and I from certain death. Swim calmly towards the outflowing current, but at 45 degrees to it, this will drift you sideways to calmer waters from where you can swim back to shore.

Chideock, a mile inland, might refer to the 10th century Saxon festival of Hoke, which celebrated the repelling of the Danes at the time of King Ethelred. 500 years later, as England embraced Protestantism, Chideock remained a staunchly Catholic enclave, centred around the Arundell family who lived in an old castle. In the 1590's, five of their priests were hanged, to be beatified in 1929 as the Chideock Martyrs nonetheless.

Chideock castle came in to its own during the Civil War when locals of both religions fought off Cromwell's fanatical Parliamentary troops. On the third attack in 1645, the handsome structure was taken by the Protestants. Typically, those extremists destroyed it and charged the Arundells £1 for so doing. Echoes of Corfe....

13 land owners lost their estates for defending the castle against General Fairfax, the Parliamentary Commander-in-Chief, who then made Chideock House (now on the busy main road) his headquarters. The old Catholic school has long since closed and local children go to the Catholic school in Bridport.

In 1685, wanting to de-throne James II, the rebel Duke of Monmouth anchored here and three of his men rowed ashore at Seatown. This advanced party failed to rouse effective support, yet a young local man who participated was later 'transported' to Barbados. Lucky him?

He might have been a fisherman. A survey in 1629 found that there were 86 fishermen in Chideock and Seatown, whilst Bridport had only 49 and Charmouth 36.

As you swing past the settlement's biggest financial sector, another caravan park, and on to the wooded path reaching uphill, try doing as locals once did. Whistle up the fairies. You might be surprised that what others take as birdsong could well be a little winged human copying your notes. If going uphill bores you, consider each step as a one-legged squat and enjoy them improving your quads and your physical and mental health.

There's a more secretive route reaching inland towards Symondsbury. A holloway. Etched into softer rock across this fair land, routes sunken up to 10 metres deep trace the tramp of our ancestors. Eight hundred, even three thousand years of footfall, hooves and rainwater has gradually submerged these tracks which are now concealed by knots of trees. Secret, unseen from three metres distant, often known only to locals, holloways are perfect escape routes. Enchanting, alluring, one falls west from Mapperton's plateau, others rise through the Marshwood Vale, many more contain roads which criss-cross Dorset and Somerset.

These enclosed trenches where antiquity touches your heart are true treasures. They are cosy places to retreat to, where, sat upon a tree root, we can settle into stable, relaxing mindsets and refresh our minds. Life is tough, even if we do not have bombs falling all around us, and it is skilful to know how to meet stress, anxiety and dissatisfaction. Settle and enjoy your body subtly shifting as your breath feeds you vital oxygen, relax as you expel air. In a flash, love being what you are, not the ego who you think you are - but your totality.

Golden Cap

golden cap etc

Off you rise up the hardened clays to Golden Cap which is a layer of greensands that are, incidentally, golden and not at all sandy. Laid down during the Cretaceous 100 million years ago, they sit on black marls, which are really soft grey mudstones. From this elevated little plateau, incredibly, one third of the time-span of complex life is evident in the cliffs you see from here.

This, the most elevated spot along England's southern coast, is an old river terrace hardened by time. The surrounding hills are flat-topped and are of this tough strata's continuation. Note repetitions in the angle of the splay of these hills and their slopes each tilted back from the coast, ruffled as if this landscape were a blanket.

100 mya

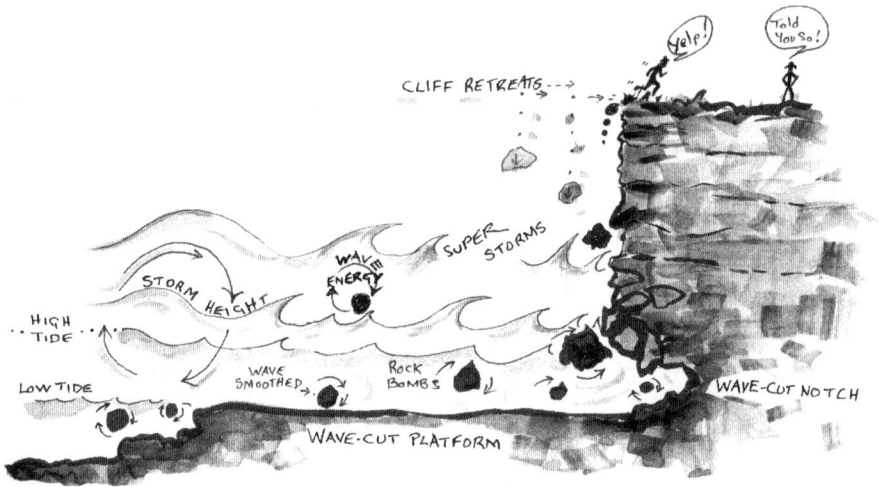

Perfectly truncated by the sea, these uplands give us amongst the richest and best exposed strata sequences anywhere, singling this coast out as a world wonder. From Golden Cap's very edge, carefully glance down to the sea and note that several arcs of rock define the retreat of this mass of land which is continually being nibbled by the waves. In time this huge bluff and these ridges will be down there forming new layers of rock upon the seabed.

It is boggling that this started before we creatures developed brains which are too big for our ethical abilities. What a fine moment to chuckle at ourselves. Accepting who we are with all of our muck and shine is quietly thrilling. We are many 'characters', one upon the other - the infant seeking attention; the stroppy or the vibrant teenager; the complicit or adventurous young adult; the staid or open semi-oldie. We shape-shifters change, dependent upon which part of our psyche we are inhabiting.

Can't keep up? Can't work out who you are manifesting as right now? Then just watch and giggle and it'll soon become clear. That's when you gain the skill of adapting and toning down, wisely easing each situation. We see that we have choice, that we can become something different. We are not our many and often conflicting little egos, these are mere spots on our surface.

The coast here has little belts of *undercliff*, wild terrain of slumped land, secret habitats beyond human reach. Skirting their tops, you pass old farm buildings and thatched cottages, the remains of a fishing village abandoned after the coast road shifted inland in 1824, all protected by the National Trust.

You rise through wild nooks, watery crannies, a lacework of ancient hedgerows, sunken lanes and rushes of woodland. There are waves of meandering fields unaltered for countless centuries, cows graze on natural grass producing equitable, environmentally friendly meat.

We need proteins but don't need to eat so much meat. It is not the individual's fault. The system has been imposed upon us. The extraordinarily fit people of the Kenyan tribe I grew up alongside, which has given us Olympian runners for decades, ate chicken once or twice a month. Beans gave them protein.

Modern vegan-ism is not squeaky clean - ripping down virgin jungle to plant soya and pulses, transporting it half way around the world, multiple layers of infrastructural support, then there's the CO_2 of heavy processing. A locally sourced, sustainable diet with less meat is a vital step in these difficult times. Though tied into this mess, we can prompt change. Our money, however little, has collective power. We can flip our economies to sustainability. In just six months Russia flipped its into a war-one. Climate Change is a war, "Like we've never seen before."

Atop the ridge at 192m, Stonebarrow, a shimmering heathland of rare plants and silver-studded blue butterflies. The blackthorn, or sloe bushes burst with song. There's the light yet assertive call of the wren turning the eye, the clear rush of a blackbird's concert piece lifts the heart, bright notes fall from the tern's beak as it darts past.

Stonebarrow's prehistoric settlement has been washed away by cliff collapses, but you can still walk in the footsteps of those Celts upon the old road which linked their homes to hill forts visible from this ridge top, the nearest being Coney, Lambert and Hardown Castles to your north. A little east are Pilsden Pen and Lewesdon hillforts.

These people, the Durotriges, a cluster of Celtic tribes, minted coins before the Roman's brutally defeated them in the year 43. Their comfortable round thatched stone huts were between 5 to 7 metres wide and they centred around sunken stone fire pits, there were stone ledges for storage, even basins for washing. There would have been storage sheds, shelters for cattle, workshops for metalworking. They ploughed and sowed oats, barley, wheat and they found food at the sea's edge. Their dead were placed crouched into oval pits with a few personal items such as pots or mirrors.

A 10 metre long boat found in Poole Harbour would have been used by the Durotriges who braved the tempestuous English Channel to trade with the French.

What we humans were and still are capable of is truly amazing.

Portland framed by Golden Cap

Charmouth beach with Golden Cap

charmouth

Slipped beneath Stonebarrow's upland lump lies Charmouth, first settled by those Celtic Durotriges whose territory reached eastwards from the River Axe to Wiltshire. The Saxons called it 'Cerne', meaning stony place and appropriately, Charmouth is known for her fossils. However, in the 1300's a living fossil terrified locals as it devoured their sheep in one gulp. This unfortunate hungry creature which they called a dragon, was killed by a knight and legend has it that the villagers renamed their settlement after him. Where are the bones of that throwback to the age of monsters? Surely they'd have been preserved in the church? Maybe they were burnt as devil bones? So much for tales of dragons, but don't tell the locals as they would only ask why you are walking the Dragon Coast.

In 1719 part of a fossilised ichthyosaur was discovered and it fitted long told tales of weirdly terrifying sea monsters. And this place has a Dragon Centre par excellence - the Charmouth Heritage Coast Centre, an astounding, free to enter little museum run by charity. Give, give, give…. Amongst many inspiring fossils enticingly displayed, there's a 4 metre long ichthyosaur which a larger reptile once killed. It took 1,000 delicate hours to prepare, you can even see its skin, which is incredible as tissue rarely fossilises.

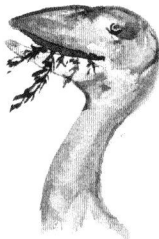

ichthyosaur - dolphin like
with crocodile snout, 4m!

These sleek pre-dinosaur marine reptiles grew to be between 4 to 10 metres long and could have two metre skulls with large eyes for hunting, their long thin snouts snapped up fast moving prey.

Fossils show ichthyosaurs congregated in shallow lagoons to give birth, granting their offspring safety in numbers away from the dangerous sea. They existed for as long as the dinosaurs, but arrived earlier, roughly 250 million years ago. The dolphin-like ichthyosaur competed with the much larger plesiosaur whose long neck whipped into shoals of squid. Pliosaurs, which we met at Kimmeridge and Weymouth Bay, grew to 15 metres, had four flippers, long thick necks and gruesome teethed heads.

Jurassic nautilus - ammonites were similar

At this time, many types of reptiles fled Pangea's extreme deserts and readapted to life in the cooler ocean. Charmouth sits by the infamous Black Ven marls which produce the soft slumping cliffs between Charmouth and the popular resort of Lyme Regis. For hundreds of years, fossils had been taken to be strange creatures from before Noah's flood.

In Dorset, ammonite fossils, especially the glistening pyrites ones, were seen as curled up snake stones and were treasured as charms by tourist and local alike. It is said St Hilda turned a plague of snakes to stone, hence their ubiquity.

Ammonites handily date rocks, for thousands of forms evolved and at very specific times. These soft-bodied squid-like creatures were protected by coiled shells that also acted as buoyancy controls. Though evolving 450 million years ago, they existed until 66 million years ago, roughly when the dinosaurs died off. Only the closely related nautilus still exists and is found in our tropical seas.

450 mya

the Cobb, reassuringly solid during a storm

lyme regis

Delightful Lyme tumbles downhill to a busy Saxon port, for Sherborne Abbey boiled salt here. She added her Regis when granted a royal charter in 1284 by Edward I. From here ships carried the coveted English wool and linen across Europe. This partly explains the plethora of handsome buildings inland - mansions, farms, barns, trading and drinking houses. Exposed to inclement weather from the SE to the SW, Lyme was an unexpected haven. Records from 1254 show that during storms, the Cobb sheltered boats from Holland, Belgium, France, even Spain and Germany.

Only Old Harry could have helped build the Cobb's perfectly engineered wall and the devil did so in exchange for the soul of the first being to walk along it. Wiser than the horned one, Lyme's townsfolk sent across a dog. Naturally angered at being deceived, the devil stamped his foot, forming a troublesome sink in the sea. But Old Harry got his own back at various times, in 1377 he swept the entire Cobb away, destroying 50 boats and 80 houses. Despite the devil's continual attacks, the hardy folk of Lyme kept rebuilding the Cobb without his aid and it seems they won, for its elegant 200 metre older arc has stood as it is now since 1539. To further annoy Old Harry, they extended it a couple of times.

The curving stone wall follows a natural basin in the rock (ha, Harry's hole?) and would at first have been a flexible, porous structure of boulders set between willow mats lashed to sunken oak piles, akin to those used to hold together Neolithic swamp 'island' dwellings. From about 1780 to 1826 the breakwater was further solidified by blocks of Portland stone floated into place tied between empty oak barrels. The stone was dovetailed with oak and iron cramps to make an immovable wall. Lyme's skilled workers were asked to build other harbours, but the Cobb is an almost unique, unaltered survivor.

Meryl Streep also defied the devil as she stood contemplating eternity in the iconic film 'The French Lieutenant's Woman', based on the book written by the local author John Fowles. Her performance bought a new wave of tourists flooding to what had once been the fossil centre of the universe.

In the 1820s, Black Ven and the strip of beach between Lyme and Charmouth became a hot spot for collecting. Along these shores superstitious tourists bought the glinting snake stones curled in tight wee knots which protected locals from evil spirits.

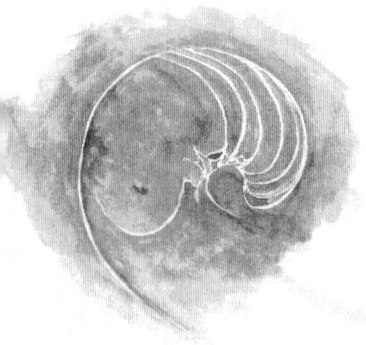

Speaking of fantasy, step westwards from the Cobb and be transported back to the time of the dinosaurs by heading along Monmouth beach. Persist over the bulbous boulders, some of which contain fossils and at low tide you will come to a wave smoothed platform adorned with swirling white designs set within the grey limestone. Your toes, so young, so tender, touch an array of stunning ammonites 200 million years old. The magic of time travelling.

Be wary when hunting fossils on Black Ven, to Lyme's east. In 2008, 400 metres of heavily saturated cliff slumped where a group of students had not long stopped collecting ammonites. A day or two afterwards, as keen fossil hunters searched this new slip for freshly exposed treasures, car-sized boulders tumbled to the beach!

upon the fabulous fossil platform

Wearing a big hat and a long dress, the famous Mary Anning scaled Black Ven to dig out fossils. Aged 34, she wrote to her friend Charlotte Murchison: "Perhaps you will laugh when I say that the death of my old faithful dog has quite upset me, the cliff that fell upon him and killed him in a moment before my eyes, and close to my feet... it was but a moment between me and the same fate."

plateosaurus feasting. 9m!

Thank goodness we didn't lose her too early, for it was slippery, muddy, dangerous work. Mary's family were known in the fossil trade for they found, cleaned and sold fine specimens. Forget the illuminated films, what story could beat that of the town's most famous person, alongside the devil of course, for it was probably in a fit of jealousy that Old Harry lashed out with a bolt of lightning, killing the woman who was holding the baby Mary, as well as the two women either side of her.

Yes, that pesky plesiosaur once again,
but first found in completeness
by Mary Anning.

That the 'Miracle Baby' survived, locals claimed, naturally made Mary Anning an incredible, intelligent and likeable child and the remarkable woman she became. Don't believe the story in the dark film in which the talented Kate Winslet skilfully portrays Mary as a miserable lump. Script writers, grrr!

Mary worked with great patience on items she unearthed, hers was the first complete plesiosaur ever found and she uncovered many other key species. Her growing body of carefully prepared work was highly regarded by geologists around the world, though the buyers/collectors, and not she herself, were often given credit.

As a self educated, working class woman, Mary Anning was lauded and respected amongst the geological elite. Yet though consulted on issues of anatomy and fossils, certain scientific men wrote papers on her original discoveries without referring to her.

Anna Pinney wrote: "...these men of learning... sucked her brains... made a great deal of publishing works, of which she furnished the contents, while she derived none of the advantages."

Mary Anning herself wrote: "The world has used me so unkindly...." Typical of the time, contributions by working-class people were credited to others of supposedly 'more elevated status'.

Yet there were influential people from major universities such as Oxford, who openly admired Mary. The highly acclaimed geologist Henry de la Beche allowed her to earn money selling his picture of prehistoric life, which he derived from Anning's vast knowledge and exquisite fossil reconstructions. She also befriended another respected fossil collector, a middle class lady called Elizabeth Philpot.

Shades of misogyny, disregard of the uneducated, tinges of racism (for country folk were seen as stupid), all blight our vision. Realising we are all equal enriches us. Genetic research has proven that everyone outside of Africa is related to a small band of just one hundred individuals who left our birth continent. That is the power of mutation, as Mary knew, it enables life to adapt to suit environmental niches.

Our skin, our eyes, they responded to available sunlight, our faces, hair and bodies adapted to each climate, creating our superb tonal and structural differences. We truly are cousins. In Africa we have more relatives, how wonderful. It is only our beliefs and attitudes which divide us. Amusingly, these were created to resolve specific issues and the lesson of evolution is that they are pliant and not cast in stone.

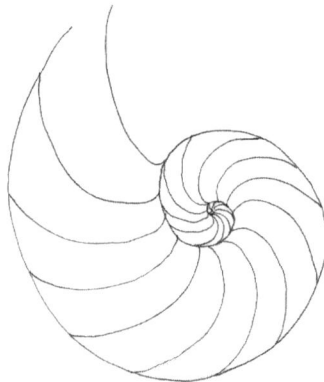

nautilus interred in Lyme's extraordinary wave-cut shelf

Metriacanthosaurus – fast, furious gobbler of anything. 8 m!

Lyme Regis Museum is built on the site of Mary's first fossil shop. Her notebook, filled with quotes and poems that were important to her, are in Dorchester Museum. Mary discovered her first fossil when she was a child. One imagines her lively character was nourished by her uneducated father, who refused to subscribe to the Articles of the Church of England. This was a serious business, such folk couldn't go to Oxford or Cambridge, nor become professionals in the Law or the Army. Not that most carpenters would have, furthermore, Mr Anning was poor due to being weakened by a fall. He died of tuberculosis in 1810, when Mary was 11.

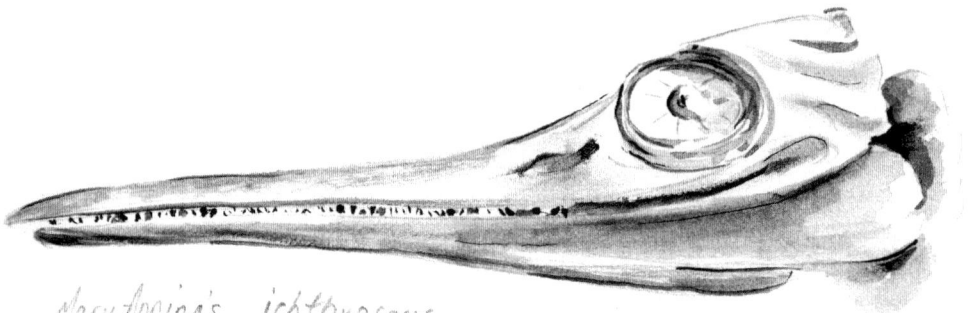

Mary Anning's ichthyosaur

It was four months later that Mary and her older brother Joseph unearthed a 2m skull belonging to a 200 million year old ichthyosaur. Mary searched and found the rest of the skeleton some months later in the cliffs, and it took over a year to clean this first complete ichthyosaur. A member of the local gentry paid the Annings £23, a huge sum and the fossil ended up in the British Museum, generating public interest in this 'Crocodile in a fossil state'.

By 1820, having made no major discoveries for a year, the family were about to sell their furniture to pay the rent when a customer called Lieutenant-Colonel T.J. Birch auctioned specimens he had purchased from the Annings and gave them

200 mya

all of the enormous sum of £400. A palaeontologist called Gideon Mantell said, "They (the Annings) have... found almost all the fine things... submitted to scientific investigation...." Buyers arrived from Paris, Vienna, everywhere, raising the family's profile in the scientific world because it was seen that their work had helped the understanding of prehistoric life.

Mary studied scientific literature and she taught herself anatomy by dissecting fish. In 1823, she found the first complete plesiosaurus, and in 1828 the first British example of a pterosaur, a flying reptile, which was displayed at the British Museum as the flying dragon. In 1829 she found a fish skeleton. In her diary, Lady Harriet Silvester described Anning as: "...thoroughly acquainted with science...in the habit of writing and talking with professors (who say) she understands more of the science than anyone else in this kingdom."

Aged 27, in 1826 she bought a house with a shop front in Broad Street and from it sold fossils to acclaimed places such as New York's Museum of Natural History, the King of Saxony was also a customer. In 1837 Mary's savings were either stolen or lost when her investor died and so she was awarded a small pension by a scientific association. Nine years later, aged only 47, she died of breast cancer.

As these facts show, Mary was loved and admired locally. Today the town's friendliness can be seen in the cheerful youth walking from school each afternoon. That is a sign that love and togetherness rule the well adjusted families whose forebears sold snakes stone, devil stones and frozen lightning bolts (bellamites to you and me), to tourists.

Years ago, a local fisherman caught a beautiful mermaid in his net and released her back into the sea, but she kept returning each time he went fishing, she even flopped along the pavements to his home. The kindly man would lead her back to the sea because he felt unable to maintain a watery relationship. She finally disappeared and, naturally, he felt sad. But then this is a town where a big black dog haunts a road at its northern edge. Maybe that dog which each night entered the home of a farmer whose wife had died, was actually the dog which beat Old Harry at his game and later decided to give a bit of joy to a lonely old man.

Lyme's small fishing fleet respectfully fishes the protected bay, they dive for scallops which are freshly cooked in the seaside stalls. Dredging, which destroys the seabed in scoop-fulls, is forbidden; deep net trawling, which devastates habitats, is banned; the number of licensed fishermen is limited. Such measures help maintain healthy stock levels. About two miles out from the sunbathers decorating the baking beaches and beyond most human contamination, rafts nurture rapidly growing mussels - the most sustainable and lowest carbon-consumptive source of protein. The mussel ropes attract many species, some of which are commercial, such as crab and lobster. If all these practices were undertaken everywhere our suffering seas might recover.

Moving east from the Cobb, you tread silky sands imported from France for the summer crowds, you'll then wobble over a shingle beach of Isle of Wight pebbles, some holding trapped fossils. Many flints have weird sculptural faces. I am convinced they are delightful story-telling spirits frozen by a cruel witch on a cold evening and that they are unlocked by charmed children who let their imaginations wander.

Rising west from this enchanted old seaside settlement, when you arrive at a spot of heathland before you walk in to a stretch of forest, look back. Let the light tease your attention. Absorb nature's abstraction of ever changing colours, the sea one hour grey, the next churned up brown, another time lightening blue or azure, calm silver, sometimes it has tinges of gold. Gold in your heart transforms what you see, a miserable mood makes a mountain monstrous, a sparkling attitude ignites a muddy puddle.

Monmouth beach, named after the thwarted rebel Duke who landed here with his army in 1685

undercliff

Between the enchantment of Lyme and the intensely farmed plateau and the popular golf course above Seaton, the path dips into miles of uncertain terrain. Striding through this patch of jungly world, be well prepared, there is no way out, only the 8 mile trek forwards with little hint of where you are. Stray from the path and if an unrecorded dinosaur doesn't get you, a crack in the ground might twist your ankle.

The Undercliff National Nature Reserve is one of the most active landslide zones in Europe. Constantly on the brink of moving, the path winds steeply through rock cavities and landslips. Useless to mankind, for nature this lost world is a haven with fallen trees coated in lichens. The South West's warm, humid climate produces temperate rainforests, few of which have survived the plough, yet here in this micro-climate, mosses, fungi and ferns exist below a dense canopy made up mainly of wild lime, beech, ash, maple as well as the invasive sycamore, all adorned with creepers galore. Tarzan would have been happy here... if he had a fur coat. There are owls and peregrine falcons, song birds, grass snakes, lizards and the great crested newt.

It all began with a thunderous whoosh on Christmas Eve in 1839, but there had been minor slips in 1775 and 1828. The 1839 slip was documented because two geologists happened to be surveying the area when it slipped, making it the first scientifically recorded landslip in the world, as well as the largest. The slump happened because too much rain seeped through the chalk, (yes, those Cretaceous chalks you thought you had left far behind), lubricating the impermeable layers of Jurassic clays below.

Celebrating such a magnificent natural event, a musical piece called the Landslip Quadrille was composed and paddle steamers played it to tourists onboard. Queen Victoria was amongst those many visitors and she particularly adored Goat Island, an isolated lump within a chasm which goats loved. She was overjoyed to learn winter wheat sown before the landslip was hand harvested the following spring.

To delight you during these 8 dark miles, there's one old sheep wash, a ruined pumping station and a tumbled down house, all of which once lay at the edge of the Rousdon Estate, which later became a private school that tutored lads from abroad, but which has now been developed into luxe housing.

The path rises from the depths to run across Goat Island's little upland block, which is mown once a year to ensure rare orchids and other flowering plants thrive in the patchy chalk grassland. This emerald world is a sensual hint of what we came from before *Homo-sapiens* evolved in the African savannah. Damp vegetation whiffs the dank air, unable to invade, the wind scoots above the canopy, the sun's intensity is far away. You are in one of Britain's few truly wild places, nothing human but your passage happens in this wilderness.

To reach out and gently swish your fingers over leaves without harming them, is one of the pleasures of being out in the countryside. Some plants release smells, others entice with their softness, some repel with sharpness or their patterned texture allures. Each sending little messages up your fingers, through your hands, into your body, up to your brain. Our thumb gives the human hand a power grip not found in other animals; the thumb-forefinger grip grants us precision, enabling us to make tools or waste away an hour pinching phone screens.

In a suitably quiet location not too near to any lurking dinosaurs, gently, voluptuously, rub your forefinger tip with the thumb, your attention tingling upon your skin. At these hyper-sensitive nodes we have more nerve endings than most creatures, granting us extreme dexterity, enabling us to wield wands, paint pictures, know if our hair needs washing. Settling into this super-sybaritic rubbing, you create a trigger to use in any stressful situation. Habituated, this action grants you rapid access to the solid security of your calm sensual core whenever you are in need. What is not to like?

Such huge cliff slumps are common along this coast, cracks in the land are often a sign that things are on the move, but there can be no warning. They happen in wet or dry weather, so do be cautious approaching cliff tops.

seaton

Popping out from the underworld at an elevation of 100 metres, you find yourself in the Great Unconformity. No, you aren't having an identity crisis. Here we have a strange mix of rocks from the Triassic, Jurassic and early Cretaceous, all tilted at an angle and then worn flat. As if that's not enough, these strata were then sunk below the sea and plastered with sediment, then, would you believe it, lifted once again to a huge height. Weathered by storms, there's rock that feels as if it ought not to be here. Imagine a layered cake, tipped, sliced, munched then licked. This odd plateau of chalk upland has not yet been slurped away by weathering, (as has much of the coastal area between here and White Nothe). Such muddled confusion is rightly called an Unconformity.

You've arrived in a contrasting world of stray golf balls upon a stretch of stray chalk upland that might remind you of the intensely farmed terrain further back in Purbeck. Scoot down Squire's Lane and spread out before you is Seaton. Yes, a bit confusing. Not that long ago we left a tiny hamlet called Seatown and here we are at a sizeable town called Seaton. Perhaps that's why the logical Romans called her "Ad Axium" due to her being at the mouth of the River Axe.

Adding further confusion, during the middle ages the people of Ad Axium preferred to sleep in what we now call Axmouth, which, bewilderingly, isn't Seaton at the river's mouth, but a settlement almost two miles inland.

They were afraid of Barbary pirates who, from the 700's onwards, whipped tens of thousands of locals off to be sold in Moroccan markets, which was well before we Brits entered the despicable and ancient people trade. Though it happened before, the first record of slavery was over 5,000 years ago. The Sumerians (Syria) openly bought and sold people, as did the Egyptians, Romans, Arabs and just about every tribe and supposed civilisation in history. And all this began before Jesus strode around Palestine. The Vikings traded people, as did tribes all over Europe and Africa. Exploiting our neighbours seems to have been de rigeur.

Those Barbary pirates taught the English well, and we soon gained infamy as pirates and as we did, the danger from abroad waned, soon houses sprouted where the Axe meets the beach. Seaton, hey presto! The expanding village continued to house fishermen and to trade wool and linen and in the 19th century, when it was fashionable to run off to seaside resorts for health benefits, the town grew rapidly.

Though Seaton's website proudly proclaims her being the inspiration for the Butlins chain of holiday camps, there are other inspiring facts. Where the train once steamed, a delightfully period tram now takes you inland to enjoy the Axe's riverside wildlife. Which is what those who lived here 6-8,000 years ago in prehistoric round houses would also have done, not the tram, but a trip up this lazy river well stocked with fish and fowl and reeds and legumes as well as an array of animals you can still enjoy seeing.

The River Axe held apart two Celtic tribes: you've met the Durotriges to the east, and there were the Dumnonia who spread all the way down to Cornwall. And the Phoenicians might well have popped in here to sample the odd apple. Seaton claims it was the Roman sea fort Moridunum. A Roman bath and an underfloor heating system were discovered here, as were 22,000 coins bearing the Roman Emperor Constantine's head. Romans gave us paved roads, they brought apples to this cider loving country, as well as asparagus, pheasants, peacocks, and guinea fowl, the brown hare and domestic cats purred in with them and due to the Romans we eat peas, celery, leeks, onions, parsnips, carrots, even cucumbers, pears and plums.

Their large ships sailed up to lovely little Colyford, where the quaint tram now stops. Early Seaton was one of the West's more important shipbuilding harbours, supplying Edward I's wars in the 1200's. Sadly, one hundred years later a huge landslip blocked the river. Eventually this water course naturally opened up once again, but never regained its importance.

In 1544 Henry VIII visited his fort on Seaton seafront, the year before he'd drunk champagne as he laid the foundations of his 'des-res' opposite Sandbanks. The town boasts the grave of the infamous smuggler Jack Rattenbury, who settled here to write his memoir before dying in 1844, content he had started the now popular celeb-autobio.

You see, anyone can write. Put this book down and begin your own. No, seriously, start a brief sunset diary spoken into your phone (which turns it to text). Recording the day's little positives enhances the mood enormously if done regularly.

In 1868 a new railway line connected Seaton to the London main line at, yes, inland Axmouth. This finally ended the transport by sea of people and goods to and from the capital and its wealthy environs. The river ferry was replaced with a low bridge in 1877 - no longer could sailors go up stream. This structure is England's oldest concrete bridge and you unwittingly crossed it on foot, with the replacement bridge (circa 1990) carrying vehicles not far from you. From here you can cycle the oddly named 'Stop Line Way', a route tracing a WW2 defensive line that reaches the Bristol Channel.

Turn inland by the tiny marina and it is just a skip, a hop and a drift along the robustly protective esplanade to the town centre. The Coastal Path also takes a skip along the prom, at least there's a final cafe to prepare yourself for the climb up White Cliff, which is the familiar Old Harry's chalk strata from way back yonder. The devil's in the detail.

The South West Coast Path is famed for buffeting gusts. On a miserable day with a howling wind, simply thinking of the insects pounded by gigantic rain bombs can help you change mindsets.

Walking a 40k pack up and down Himalayan ridges was a weird joy in the relentless monsoons. Bridle paths became raging streams, soaked to the skin, boots filled with muddy liquid, leeches creeping up my legs, miles to trudge before I could erect my tent. Old pop favourites hummed deeply with the drum beat of rain drops kept me going. Soon the sun shone from within, bright mindsets eased my weary wet way.

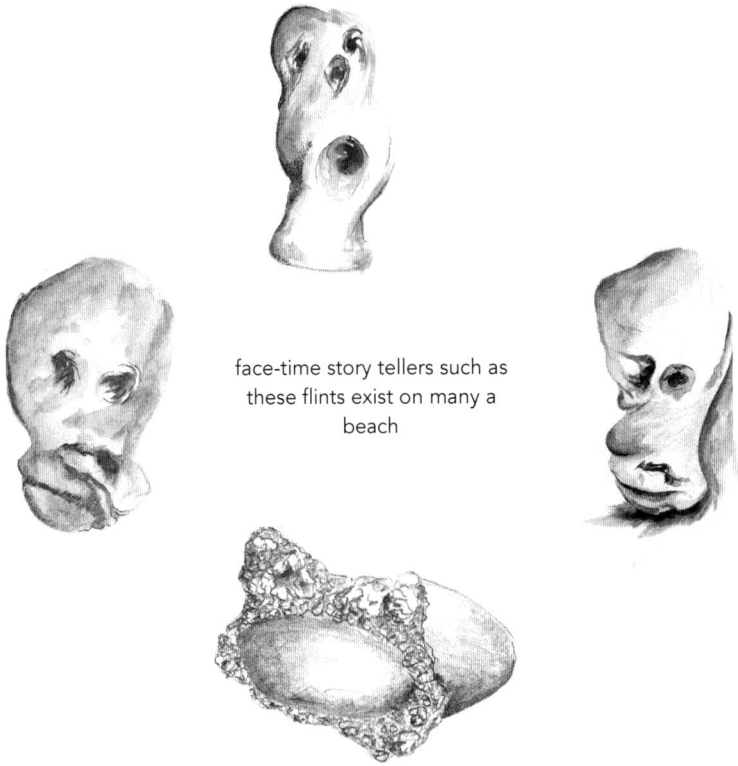

face-time story tellers such as
these flints exist on many a
beach

there's even the odd stone eating frog washed along from Budleigh Salterton

With a hum, what a marvel the drenched British landscape, drips falling off leaves, waves ripping rocks, wind speeding birds, horizons bursting with purple storms. Eye-video such wonders and store them in your mind. Ha, life on the run! If you seek shelter and there's no lightning, the beech is better than the chestnut, followed by the oak, but the ash leaks dribbles down your neck.

beer

Cuddled in a tight valley some steep strides above a pebble beach, a suspended fishing village with an improbable magic drew Victorian tourists from Seaton and further afield. It has always been like this. Them stone-age folk who settled near what later became a hill fort high up on the ridge above, waddled their way down the stream. Near what is today Bovey House, on their way back uphill, they sat to eat oysters, mussels and fish and even lugged back sizeable flints to work in their settlement upon the ridge.

Throughout the ages, to be a man, boys had to plunge into this stream which now courses down the main street. As the settlement grew, the stream stank of gutted fish guts, until a Victorian woman paid for it to be cleaned up and canalised.

The hardy sailors of Beer launched their fishing boats off the lovely pebble beach and, using a hand turned capstan, 20 men winched them up the shingle; today it's a push of a button. The women, who washed the fish they'd gutted from their nimble hands, were renowned for high quality lace, some of which decorated Queen Victoria's wedding dress in 1840. They had been taught this lucrative craft by Flemish refugees who arrived here in the 17th century.

Beer fishermen were widely admired for handling their 10 metre luggers and when not quarrying or fishing, many a man smuggled and by 1750, the area was notorious. As one reporter stated, "Beer men were the very kings of smugglers." Beer was a fine spot to land and transport silk, tea, tobacco and brandy, brought over from Alderney or the French coast. We've already met celeb-autobio, Jack Rattenbury, who was born in Beer.

He stored kegs of brandy he had bought in the Channel Islands, deep in Beer Quarry's caves before selling them throughout East Devon. Not all Beer men were smugglers, some worked to catch them, which proved difficult as they often were bribed to turn a blind eye, but they were rewarded if contraband was handed to the authorities, who sold it on. As you can imagine, this too was a tempting way for customs officials to make money....

Old Harry's chalks have reappeared to decorate the western beach with a sculptural creamy pleasure of a cliff washed by waves. A little inland, another load of Cretaceous strata laid down in bands 5 metres broad, gave Roman Beer it's raison d'être. Laid 120 million years ago in lush swamps, Beer Stone emerges damp but soon dries hard, hence it is ideal for detailed carving, such as interior church features. This durable stone decorates Exeter, Westminster, St Paul's and 21 other cathedrals.

Today tiny little Beer, littered with crabbing boats and selling crab sandwiches, attracts more visitors than you could fit in to a reasonable resort, which shows in the eateries and shops. Would you believe it, even though some a distance from railway lines, she also houses Pecorama, the world's leading manufacturer of model railway systems. Their lovely gardens are a tourist attraction and tea can even be had in an old railway carriage. How, one wonders, did they get it here? Ask those hardy fisher folk.

an
incomplete
drag of incomplete tracery from K92
Beer Museum

Feet firmly on the solid path, cheeks registering the salty air, eyes absorbing light reflected from the sea, ears tuning in to the natural sounds, your fundamental being awakes. Stirred by simply being without agenda, just floating on the eternal now as it unfolds, is an elemental experience, it is soothing and satisfying.

the 1790 landslip, Hoken Cliff, west of Beer

branscombe

Scooting westwards, you can dip in to more undercliff or walk beside intensely farmed chalky fields. Whichever you choose, if you make it to the end, enjoy the view over Branscombe Vale's random pattern of medieval fields. Due to the terrain, industrial high tech farming is impossible. Older meadows enclosed by hedgerows follow streams and old paths, cows munch nutrient rich grasses, wild flowers and herbs growing in complex, healthy soils fertilised by their manure for centuries. Such old-fashioned husbandry is a sustainable beacon in this uncertain epoch when chemicals, fertilisers and monstrously heavy tractors have all but killed our once fecund soils.

On those nature favourable farms found in the many valleys reaching back from the sea, curving hedgerows can be medieval, some near to hill forts can be as old as 3,000 years, that is back to the Bronze Age. You can date them yourself. Count the number of different species of shrubs and trees in a 30m stretch, that's 30 grand strides. One species will take hold roughly every 100 years, so ten species in 30 good paces equals 1,000 years. Near here, I recently counted 17.

There's more rectangular fields on the plateau higher up. This can often indicate where open common land was taken over by landlords between 1780 and 1840. Yet they could also be the result of modern farmers removing 'troublesome' hedgerows for 'greater efficiency'.

Should the weather be clement, you may wish to relax at Branscombe beach's cafe. The village is also a welcome and logical night halt for walkers.

One sunny dawn in 1941, having flattened the centre of old Plymouth a few minutes flight west, a Nazi pilot dropped his last remaining bomb near Branscombe Radar Station. Exhausted after a long nightshift, my mother wasn't woken by the explosion. Her deep dreams were ended when her amazed comrades emerged from the air-raid shelter and shook her awake. My blessed mother was sometimes mocked by hardy fishermen in various villages and towns as she gave 'War pep-talks' which were part of an officer's duties.

About 4 miles westwards, as you dip down to Weston beach, you'll find terrain typical of that seen by our most ancient of ancestors - a patchwork of woodland and open vales. Having gained the ability to walk on two legs, *Sahelanthropus* wandered through half open savannah glades at the edges of forests. That was about 7 million years ago. About 2 million years ago, *Homo-erectus* left Africa to arrive in the Middle East, and fade out. Roughly 8-10,000 years ago *Homo-Sapiens* finally found the Jurassic Coast.

That took a lot of ingenuity. An intelligence capable of coping with new, unfamiliar environments; tools; a mainly meat diet; an efficient striding gait. Walking upright is quite something. Seen from the side, your heel forms a circle as it lifts, moves forwards and drops to the ground. So efficient.

To further celebrate the multiple marvels which brought us this far in evolutionary terms, be awed as you move atop these cliffs that we humans also walk on two legs! Since dinosaur sped about with elegance, few living creatures stride for more than a few paces, ostriches and gibbons being some of the exceptions. Apes swagger and wobble awkwardly from leg to leg, whilst our gait is smooth and highly efficient.

But don't get too big headed, the Jesus lizard and penguin are quite fast. Regardless, relish the mechanical spectacle of stepping out and keeping upright as you chuckle at robots trying to mimic your deftness. As you roll onwards, enjoy the technical marvels throughout your body - the interplay of limbs, muscles, tendons and bones propelling you in the most efficient manner. We humans can out 'marathon' most animals if we drink enough.

Aware of this magical invention which took over seven million years to perfect, gain gusto from your inbuilt mechanics and be gleeful that you are utterly human!

towards Sidmouth from Ladram Bay

sidmouth

The red cliffs adorning both ends of Sidmouth's beach tell you that it's bye, bye Jurassic, hello Triassic. Well, you could have sung that song as you left Seaton, and then again at Branscombe, but this magical seaside town deserves a song.

Before we do, before you plunge the 160 metres into this charmed resort, keep your eyes peeled for peregrine falcons. You may also wish to walk 800m inland and see where helium was first detected in the sun by the man who set up the scientific journal 'Nature'. Norman Lockyer's observatory later revealed geomagnetic secrets to a strange scientist called Donald Barber, who believed in alien life forms, so tread carefully in case Old Harry is lingering behind the odd cluster of star gazing domes!

Lovely Sidmouth, a small fishing village in the 12th century, wasn't always genteel. The Old Ship Inn, built in 1350, served cider to Jack Rattenbury, our pen wielding smuggler who was also associated with the infamous Mutter family of Ladram Bay, after whom Mutter's Moor overlooking Sidmouth might well be named. This ought not stop you relaxing in the elegance of the Regency town's refined streets which boast over 500 listed buildings... as well as a favourable microclimate.

There are apple orchards in the hills reaching back from the coast so do enjoy a fresh-pressed apple juice, or perhaps a cool local cider. In the late 1650's, South West cider makers discovered that thicker bottles allowed gases to develop without the glass shattering. The 'English Method', as the technology was then called in France and elsewhere, enabled Dom Pérignon, a French wine-making monk, to perfect older sparkling methods which were in use in the south of France and thus create the much loved champagne sipped upon Sandbank's modern terraces.

There's more than two families here making still and bubbly ciders and many more in the interior. These are not industrial ciders, which are bubbled up water and chemical flavours with the odd apple thrown in, these are drinks you sip rather than glug and they are made with care and expertise in small barns. When well made, these ciders are often single-variety treats. Do ask around and find a pub which serves the proper stuff and taste those available until you get one that is as fine as a good wine.

Perhaps the poet Laureate, John Betjeman was sipping one when he wrote of Sidmouth: "A town caught still in a timeless charm." Maybe it is due to those ciders that Sidmouth is a regular winner of Britain in Bloom.

fossilised bones in a local stone

Cider and ale-happy folk, rather than drunk skunks, can be found in this elegant town for ten days in August as the charmed streets team with authentic musicians, traditional dancers and story tellers from around the world. A stage in the park presents Georgian singers, Tibetan dancers, Gambian drummers, as well as colourful Morris dancers from around the corner. They take over hotel lounges, pubs and pavements, they pop up everywhere, delighting the ears with joyously spontaneous solo or group performances.

The folk festival climaxes with a magical torchlight procession through the town. No fossils here, but living traditions well loved.

Sidmouth Museum has fossilised fragments of the hardy creatures which survived Triassic Devon's harsh deserts. Along the western seafront the cliff face has revealed fish and reptiles of this tough era, as well as evidence of labyrinthodonts, a strange amphibian like a huge flat headed frog, as well as other toothy, long-mouthed beasts deriving from primitive reptiles, from which dinosaurs were to evolve.

A coffee or a cider could help you to cope with the steep hill ahead and may even inspire glimpses in those Triassic deserts. As you gaze at the stunningly red cliffs, marvel that you who evolved from a relationship between a mitochondria and a nucleus, have evolved into the strangest of creatures who loves cafe-life. Your origins can be traced back through female hereditary mitochondria to a single woman, the original Eve! We mammals who left the birds well behind in their dinosauric state, can look up and enjoy the gulls' skilful twisting and turning above these red Triassic cliffs. If the wind is high, Jonathan Livingstone Seagull will be performing masterful acrobatics as he glides through the air's forces. Seagulls perfectly define the present moment, they remind us that we are each better than we imagine we are.

The path west touches the edge of Mutter's common, a bulk of heathland, like Studland's, that has hardly changed since ancient man settled this ridge. Leaving this inspiring terrain with its old woodlands, we wander past large fields once common land where locals once grazed their livestock, harvested wood, fungi, herbs and hunted wild creatures. At Ladram Bay you skirt a mini-town of 400 caravans and you could dip down for a picnic upon the sands and admire, sketch or snap the red rock stacks so beautifully carved by waves. The seemingly solid cliff behind you will gradually be decimated into such stacks as time goes passes.

extinctions

We have already touched on the most recent and rapid extinction which ended the Cretaceous period 66 million years ago. However, it has been found that this great dying started 25,000 years earlier. Volcanic eruptions in India caused hyperthermal warming, expelling CO_2 and SO_2 (sulphur dioxide) and generating acid rain (just like modern pollution). As plants and creatures struggled to survive, those minute coccoliths had their work cut out generating oxygen.

Another much slower extinction lasting about 15 million years, culminated in the Triassic's end roughly 210 million years ago. Enormous volcanic eruptions in what is now the mid-Atlantic, but was then central Pangea, spewed out CO_2 and SO_2, gradually poisoning the atmosphere, slowly killing off 80% of oxygen loving life. This was similar to a much larger extinction 42 million years previously, which began when Siberian volcanic eruptions ended the Permian period with noxious gases that, with subsequent climate change creating the Big Freeze, eradicated 95% of life and is rightly called the Great Dying. And long before then, roughly 365 million years ago, there had been the Devonian Extinction which wiped out 75% of all things, which, at that dastardly time, were mostly in the cooler, more habitable sea. Before that there was the Ordovician one 440 million years ago. There might have been others, but lifeforms were too tiny and frail to leave any record.

Earth seems not to want pesky life-forms itching her skin!

66

210

252

365

440 mya

Devon's luscious red cliffs were created during the Triassic, when we would have been able to ride fleet-of-foot dinosaurs right across the 12,000 mile breadth of Pangea. Imagine galloping from northern Norway to Argentina's Cape Horn, as well as from San Francisco to Hong Kong. In one gigantic lump, the Americas, Antartica, Africa, Eurasia and Australia, with East Asia just hanging on. This was a vast continent whose iceless poles and seaboards were covered in warm forests, but whose centre was mostly rainless, dry and harsh, creating deserts like none in existence today. This is why the rock is red: ferric oxide coats grains of sand in deserts and these ancient effects can be seen in the western United States and in the Red Sandstone of Europe.

Reptiles often left the land for the sea* and gradually over the first 20-30 millions years of the Triassic, various reptiles, who all breathe air by the way, crept back out from the sea. On the recovering fringes of the extinction-devastated land, they thrived on the abundance of insects in the recovering vegetational cover near the vast single ocean.

250 mya

*interestingly, the first known fossil drawing was of a plesiosaur bone in 1605

Roughly 240 million years ago, the first dinosaurs appear. The elegantly formed coelophysis could cope with the harshness. Agile two-footed lizard-like dinosaurs, they had sharp teeth and grasping hands, they thrived by eating the huge insects and smaller insect gobbling reptiles and over 20 million years, they grew to measure 3-4 metres from head to tail.

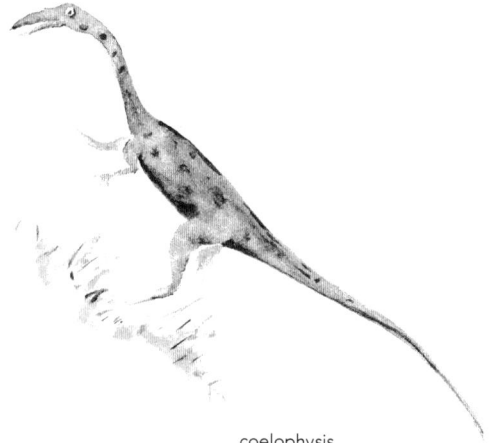

coelophysis

By 228 million years ago the delicate pterosaurs took to the sky. They would evolve to have 15m wingspans. That's as wide as three modern terraced houses.

and it's skeleton as found

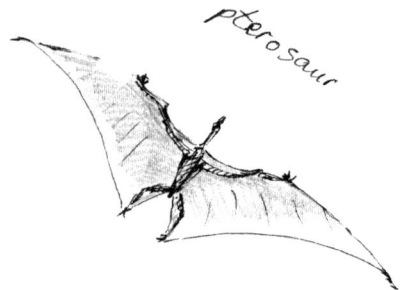

pterosaur

225 million years ago, reptiles called synapsids produced creatures called mammaliaformes, small, nocturnal insect gobblers from whom mammals would one day emerge.

Throughout the Triassic, new and bigger species evolved amongst the reptile-dinosaurs. The dinosaurs diversified to become much larger by the middle-end of the Triassic, prosauropods are an example. Roughly 90 million years later, in the Cretaceous herds of iguanodon evolved. These 10 metre long hind-legs sprinters ate copious amounts of ferns, conifers and the tough cycads which they digested in their huge bellies. They were attacked by savage headed and sharp toothed theropods, called land sharks because they tore off chunks of flesh and couldn't chew (much like the pliosaurs). In response, natural selection gradually evolved the scelidosaurus, a well armoured beast.

And then they all died out one way or another about 66 million years ago. The power of genetic adaptation has created the amazing array of species populating this beautiful planet, but we are in the Anthropocene, an all too familiar era during which we humans have the power of the gods in ours hands.....

Despite Earth's attempts at getting rid of us, life has produced cider makers. Whether you've been star spangled or not, climb to the elevated enchantment of Connaught Gardens and proceed to relish the impressive views from Jacob's Ladder just beyond.

How easy to walk these well trodden, carefully maintained paths. Once a curious beast loving the freedom of the untrod wilds, I now realise our brutal passage is best held upon tracks, for they protect the multitude of hidden creatures surrounding us. Talking of which, spotting a lumbering beetle threatened by your heavy foot fall - pause, adore it. Using a fallen leaf, gently lifting it aside and placing it away from harm's way will give you a buzz. You've saved a life!

A wild flower meadow, of which there are now 90% fewer than there were in 1950, is a boon. Not only does it provide a superb ecosystem in which a myriad of small creatures can flourish, but it sequesters carbon as organic biomass accumulates and degrades to be locked into the knotted root systems. This is not released into the atmosphere, which happens when a tree dies.

A wild meadow captures double what a typical woodland does. Converting to flower meadows the 2 million heavily fertilised and chemically sprayed hectares that feed livestock with barley and wheat, that's 40% of all arable land, would be a huge boon, as we reduce livestock numbers. That is flower-power supreme.

Enjoy your breath doing its own thing, flowing in and out. It is magical, it is keeping you alive. Being with it is relaxing. Being with your physical self is satisfying. The more we do so, the better, the stronger it becomes… and making it part of existence is fulfilling.

budleigh etc

Turning from the lazy River Otter's sea snout, which, in order to cross, you must chase a wooded track inland to a bridge over half a mile away. You'll be entertained by salt marsh flora with glasswort, sea purslane and sea lavender as well as birdsong erupting from dense vegetation.

This river's end, once improved for agriculture, is now remodelled to absorb storm flooding and allow saline water which has attracted lost plants and species. More attention to our rivers is vital. Privatising our water gave investors enormous profits but fouled our fresh waters with sewage, our beaches and seas too. The hormones and pills we take for our health, flushed here, affect every living creature, even stopping fish from reproducing.

If you wish, your physical effort can be rewarded by Budleigh Salterton's artful street of cafes and beach outlets. Budleigh, one more jewel in the string of classic English seaside resorts this path has provided. As her name hints, salt has been harvested here since before Julius Caesar invaded these isles. However, a few centuries later, fearing Viking raiders and those enslaving Barbary pirates, people lived almost two miles inland at East Budleigh. The settlement was later visited by the Norman accountants who, in their Doomsday Book, noted:

"Land of King William. Bodelie. Households: 16 villagers. 20 smallholders. 4 slaves. 10 others. 13 plough-lands. 12 men's plough teams. Meadow 5 acres. Pasture 100 acres. Woodland 20 acres. 2 cattle. 12 sheep. Annual value to lord: 10 pounds in 1086; 10 pounds when acquired by the 1086 tenant-in-chief in 1086: King William. Lord in 1086: King William. Lord in 1066: King Edward."

From Open Domesday Org, by Anna Powell-Smith.

Almost five centuries after the Normans' accounting, in 1552, Sir Walter Raleigh was born in a manor which still stands not far from here. This Elizabethan pirate-cum-hero-cum-rascal excelled in hauling other people's ships and goods homewards, so it wasn't just the barrels of sherry he stole from Cadiz which flooded London's pubs that made him rich. Angering Queen Elizabeth, he secretly married Bess, her Lady-in-Waiting, but he quickly enchanted the Queen with his vibrant personality. Surprising the historical novelist Hillary Mantel, who settled in Budleigh, never wrote about Raleigh. She came here after writing Wolf Hall and continued writing more historical works, enjoying these Jurassic views.

Budleigh's beach level prom-cum-path has a surprise in store. Behind the row of beach huts reaching eastwards, in the low red cliff, a panel indicates where you can see fossilised tree roots. Treasure this, as it is one of the few places they can be seen safely, unless you are a rabid rock climbing geologist, or had dropped down to the western end of Ladram Bay beach, 3 miles back down the coast. Solidified minerals lifted by roots created these frozen sculptures which take you back to rivers that ran from mountains (in today's France) and across the Triassic deserts 245 million years ago.

245 mya

Within the imposing red Triassic cliffs to Budleigh's west, you can see desert sands honeycombed by weathering. If you look carefully, you'll also see a fine example of a fault where these bands are distorted, one thrown up, the other down. There are also clearly defined bands of pebbles.

a ray's egg purse

Sit on the beach and run your fingers over the pleasing oval pebbles, each so perfect, smooth and tactile. A fossil in a quartzite pebble dates this rock to having been laid down as deposits in a sea 443 million years ago. That original seabed was solidified and then lifted to form mountains in a desert. Millions of years of flash floods broke up those hard slopes, tumbling rock, rounding boulders, eventually depositing smoothed pebbles in a band 30m deep, 4 miles wide (now stretching up to Minehead on the north coast). The sea here battered these cliffs, dislodged the pebbles and wave action littered this and other beaches all the way back to Portland with their beauty. That's the simple and not incorrect answer.

Rubbed against your cheek, a skin smooth pebble, an ancient stone enjoyed by a wonderful being whose life span is yonks less than it took to make a tiny scratch on this time-travelling orb. This, your ephemeral connection to this vastness of time.

Climb up the path, exit a small woodland, keep your head down past another golf course and step along shallow red ridges artfully truncated by the sea. Red falling onto perfect little pocket beaches designed for seals rather than spade and bucket. The climb eases as you approach the local summit of a 128 metres elevation at West Down with views 40 miles eastward to Portland across a bay which has been yours for half

443 mya

of this trek. Look back, count the bands of creamy rock, ten or more each laid down over millions of years between the ongoing red, but why white? It was the same sun-baked sandy material set down without oxygen at the foot of lakes and wide rivers, for oxygen rusts, releasing the inherent red iron. The strata slopes downwards towards the east, more proof that the continents tipped.

You move onwards over this deepest of deserts far, far worse than any on Earth today, your techno-boots treading back before Madame T-Rex romped around this land we now call England. Incredibly rare Triassic fossils in these sandstone cliffs offer a glimpse of survivors of the Permian extinction, there are fragments of bone and teeth from rauisuchians, extinct creatures related to crocodiles which could grow up to 6 metres long. They may have occupied the top of the food-chain in the Triassic's post-extinction deserts for munched prey lie amongst their five-toed footprints. However, agile three-toed dino-reptiles soon began to compete with them, those first little proto-dinosaurs called coelophysis.

Slipping round to the end of this walk, here stands the last caravan park, another expanse of excitement for city dwellers for whom such holidays open up possibilities and horizons which will forever inspire their children. Taking an inner city group across a field on one of the weekend trips I ran, a lass shouted, "Sir! You've brought us through a cow's toilet!" Suppressing a giggle, I watched those teenagers in shining trainers hold their noses as they avoided widely spaced cowpats. Some of those tough, anti-establishment, streetwise youths who would test-fight me, began to avoid gang culture. They carved out positive futures as youth leaders or teachers of outdoor activities. Some might have been up on this headland by the holiday park, aiming their army rifles at targets, whilst below on the sandy beach, their friends' children made sandcastles.

We are often caught in the mould our environment has created. It can take a jolt to get out of the rut. It is easier to use the tool nature has given - the more you are attentive of your body, the more your brain links with its movement and position in space, the more settled in your own niche you become. Our primordial being exists aside of thought's force, it is powerful, it charges you. If you let this process continue, you inhabit profound, stable mindsets which remodel you. Don't imagine a superstar shining on a stage, for your vigour will be silent, humble, yet heartfelt. From here, autonomy gradually arises, you sense a way forwards.

exmouth

It is a short skip along a low cliff to Orcombe Point, the official start or culmination of the Jurassic Coast Path. As that is the best place to end this book, we will return in a few pages, having wandered a wee bit up the Exe estuary.

Rounding the lump of Straight Point you can see how this red buffer, along with the distant bulks of Portland and Prawle Point, have held back the worst ravages of easterlies and westerlies. The Exe has lugged along yillions of zillions of tonnes of sand and soil stolen from the interior and laid it down as sediments that will one day become rock strata. And nature's given you an example here in these cliffs: delicious layers of cake-like rock sculpted over the centuries. A tsunami wave generated by a glacial lake in the North Sea breaking its banks, carved out the English Channel, flooded the Exe and the River Frome. These rivers each owe their width to rising sea levels as the ice melted 10-12,000 years ago. Such features are delightfully called rias and the Exe is one of several adorning the South West coastline.

The estuary and the curling tip of sand called Dawlish Warren over the far side, has for millennia been a secure stop-over for thousands of migrating birds and a sublime haven for those over-wintering here. The shallow expanse of saline water abounds with worms and molluscs, attracting many waders, it is rightly an acclaimed nature reserve protected from foaming Atlantic surf by Dawlish's rare double-sand-spit backed by sand dunes.

It is worth taking the lower path from the pillar celebrating the Jurassic Coast and stepping down the wooden incline to the beach. You arrive upon a stretch of North America! Well, Pangean America some 200 million years ago when all this excitingly red rock was laid down. Carved by aeons of wild winters and blistering summers, this seemingly solid strata is exposed so you can admire strips of the almost ivory rock we saw earlier.

As you leave the ideal beach where the estuary merges with the sea and step along the long promenade towards Exmouth marina, sniffing the estuary air, you might note the precise spot, on your specific day, where the salty smell of the sea is taken over by the organic sniff of brackish water. Passing the last sunbather, if it's the season, you will soon arrive at a seaside town boasting a find of Byzantine coins from about 400CE.

The Exmouth area suffered neglect under the thumb of Exeter, once Countess Wear was built near that dominant city in 1272 by the Countess of Devon, Isabella de Fortibus. The weir earned the Countess's family good money for centuries as they harvested taxes from every barge or craft that passed by. Many of these were filled with Devonian wool, amongst a haul of other exportable and importable goods.

In the 1200's, John the Miller built a windmill at Exmouth to harvest the south-west winds. A 12th century landing called Pratt, seasonal docks built in the 1500's and the ferry across the Exe turned a small cluster of farms into a town. But the folk suffered raids by what they called 'Turkish pirates' - those Barbary pirates who sold locals as slaves in North Africa.

Exmouth claims to be England's oldest seaside holiday location. As Napoleon burned Europe, the wealthy found solace taking the sea salts at Exmouth, attracting Lady Byron, even Lord Nelson's wife is buried here. However, in 1861, plebs such as us common folk arrived en mass on the newly constructed railway line. High class tourism wilted and what Exmouth classes as its 'golden age' created what is a mainly Victorian town, with the odd Georgian building amongst the plethora of lovely Edwardian homes. Today the town is a centre for water sports such as kite sailing and wind surfing; it has also become a foodies hotspot with several inspiring places tempting you to relish fine food fussed over in greatest detail.

Confronted with the dazzling splay of goods enticing us in every urban setting, in every supermarket, a part of us wakes up and asks why so much excess, why are we addicted to it? It is not our fault. Since we were born, the power of consumerism has, drip by drip, defined what we assume we need. It defines what we think we must identify with, what we must have to feel whole. Christmas, a consumptive web spun around us since childhood, is its zenith.

Buying excess is 'retail therapy', is ego boosting.

"I me me mine," sang George Harrison when fed up with his ego in 1969. He soon realised he was bigger than, "Old blabber mouth...."

Nonetheless, Exmouth is championing the environment. The campaign group Surfers Against Sewage awarded the town Plastic Free status in 2020. 28 local businesses have stopped using or producing single-use plastics. Each year the town holds the popular Plastic Free Festival. If you are an early walker, at 8.30 each Sunday morning, the beach is combed for plastic and rubbish and in 2023, 1,500kg were collected. Living consciously, living collectively has energised the community. This is happening across the country, across Europe, around the world, groups small and large are working towards sustainability. Where our governments and businesses fail us, we the collective individuals are showing that we can protect this precious, unique planet.

A local cuttlefish, whose 'bone' I found on the beach. One of the squid family which predate us by 250 million years. Increased CO_2 is turning the sea more acidic, threatening this species arguably more intelligent than a human infant.

orcombe point

An eternity of change,
subtle, ever shifting, this
walk has shown us. Looking
back from this pillar of rock
made of strata from this magical
coast, let your mind wander From
Exmouth to Studland. A list of
beautiful, exceptional and rare
physical features each the result of
aeons of alteration. 90 miles of human
yesterdays and enticing todays; intriguing
tales, charmed settlements and complex
agrarian patterns splattered with ecological
gems.

A long list of caring individuals and groups along
this route have fed us, sheltered us, harvested their
produce for us, they have tended the paths and
routes we have used. Having trekked across 250 million
years Orcombe Point's triangular 'Geo-needle', an
elegantly simple construct erected to celebrate ancient
marvels such as ammonites and Madame T-Rex. Its shiny
cousin, also by Michael Fairfax, delights a shopping street in
Exeter.

What excitement Exmouth's refined excesses would have
generated thosewho came and went from southern England as the
climate changed from Mediterranean to ice and back several times.

700,000 years ago a species of humanoid left stone tools and footprints in East Anglia, a fleeting visit from *Homo-antecessor* who loved Spain as much as modern Brits. England even has hints of Neanderthals who preferred mainland Europe until they mysteriously disappeared as our presence expanded. Leaving Africa roughly 60-70,000 years ago, a small clan of the latest *Homo-sapiens*, expanded in all directions, increasing their numbers in the agreeable Mediterranean, some of their off-spring loved fecund France. A few buried one of their group in East Anglia 30,000 years ago. The body was ceremonially coated in ochre, showing that they might well have loved Exmouth's shops. Other weather immune clans walked to here as the glaciers retreated.

Homo heidelbergensis. (copy of Smiths own reconstruction) pronounced eye brows, small cranium yet human

Here's an interesting thought to mull over: Dinosaurs dominated the land for about 165 million years, but couldn't draw. Yet we humans who 3.5 million years ago were shifting from being ape-ish creatures, move pencils across paper, our finger tips manipulate smart-phone cameras. How come we evolved so rapidly? Cider, cheese? No. Our unique thumb-forefinger grip enabled tools. Walking and language developed our brains. And fire - cooking avails more energy from food to feed our greedy brains. And , naturally, there's more….

Orcombe Point's apparent solidity will become another set of eroded stacks such as those at Ladram Bay and Old Harry's crew. Our thoroughly preoccupying present era is but a fleeting moment in geological time's vast expanse so upon these red cliffs, it might be a fitting culmination to take a moment to consider what you have got your head around as you walked, paused and marvelled.

Since these red sands were last blown by desert winds, three devastating extinctions failed to stop evolution's dogged progress. The vitality within every cell of every creature which lived before the last drastic day 66 million years ago, enabled new life forms to begat newer ones. Despite the odds, the merciless processes of natural selection continued through millions of years, each unexpected surviving aberration gained a slight advantage, each successful feature flourished, be it the shape of a bone, the texture of skin, the lens of an eye.

And, hey presto!
You. Me.
We.

Well, we,

the dinosaurs' heirs, magicians who long ago crafted shoes to protect our feet, can now construct rockets to soar beyond meteors such as that which killed off T-Rex and Co.

We,

who might fly off to a Triassic planet far less pleasant than this, exist within a complex web of delicate ecosystems that we barely understand, each so fragile that the shampoos we use can be devastating. A frangible framework tipping towards total catastrophe... it has happened before, as we know. As we've seen, it's a fluke we are reading these pages.

Yet there's hope. Exmouth is showing us how to manage precious environments; Lyme Bay is being cared for by fishermen and locals; Studland is well managed; and more.... Costa Rica has made itself an environmental haven, Indonesia is protecting its coral havens. The list goes on.

Unwittingly programmed to lavishly consume by a culture that worships profit and GDP (gross domestic production), we are conditioned to feel happy when our personal existence matches the Barbie model of materialism. Our ego identifies with stuff, ergo, the Planet sighs. Yet Bhutan measures itself against GDH - Gross Domestic Happiness.

"You have enjoyed a beautiful world. My generation can't. It is being destroyed for profit," a frustrated young woman exclaimed at one of the many, many, too many...

Global Warming conferences amusingly called COPs.

How to turn this tide?

It is quite simple.

We each have the power to control the world by our choices. Our money is potent. If today we were all to buy sustainably, next week, feeling the effect, industries would respond, for they are profit driven. And everything we do can help the Planet.

Fat King Henry of the many wives could never have dreamed of even the lowest living standard that we in the West have taken for granted for decades. We don't need such luxury. Every act, every production process consumes energy, buying less, doing less, enjoying simply existing is the way, the sane satisfying way. The Earth's ecological systems are groaning. In such a short time, we've left only 5% of the Planet unaltered. A revolution, not just out there, but in our attitudes is desperately needed.

We are capable of this. Our desires are fuelled by what we tell ourselves. GDHappiness is to be at ease with ourselves, regardless of our circumstances*. And it is oddly fulfilling.

A comforting breath,
enjoy being inside the universe's most amazing bit of kit.
What treasure! The luck to exist in this moment.
That's GDH, the silent power which can transform world
economies, and quickly.
'They' won't, it is not in their interest,
but we can.

Living lightly we can save the Planet.
Clichéd, but true.

* interested or doubtful? Read P216

That's the rub.
Living lightly starts by admiring you - the universe's greatest
wonder. You, a highly complicated world of cells, each with its
own task, each relating to its neighbours as they all dance in
synchrony to generate life.
Your life.

Let this appreciation give you strength. Enjoy being the bigger,
broader, more responsible, most wonderful you. You, delicate
yet powerful, the product of 3 billion years of
knife-edge hustling and innovation.

Valuing what we actually are, what we have,
we sense our place in the enormity of things,
we know our potential.

Upon this walk we have seen that we humans are capable
of just about anything.
We are the creature that can preserve nature,
for we think,
we empathise,
we love.
We act.

looking back along the wonder coast

for what it's worth,

we are more capable than we imagine.
To demonstrate this, a personal note might be helpful.

This book arose because I needed a challenge. A mind scrambled by seizures, mini-strokes, near-death health-incidents; suffering from brain fatigue it could hardly grasp the page it had just written.

Near my home lies the Jurassic Coast and writing meaningfully about the area involves comprehending several complex subjects. Simplifying these and making them enjoyable as well as adding in a little environmental awe and some self-respect made this an inspiring, though taxing project to undertake when unwell.

A year later, I think this addled mind can hold much of the book (though not all facts and names). The artwork had a similar curve - at the start I could hardly draw nor paint, though I have done so since childhood.

We have the power to not be dragged down by most situations. We can change calcified habits and attitudes, we can act to recover our lost selves.

We simply need to know it. And we can do much more. We can help to save the Planet. All this is done in manageable steps.
It takes application, it requires consistency.
Soon it becomes a joy.

loose references

Copious notes for this book were from an amalgamation of hundreds of searches, scientific, historical and otherwise.

Type an item into your search engine *and* discriminate.

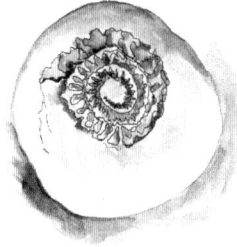

thanks to

my advisor, editor-in-chief and inspiration - Millie my wife, who has suffered endless questions, debates, re-reads, re-edits. Sarah Hanmer for your extensive proof-reading and thoughts; Dr Paul Davis, Geology Curator, Lyme Regis Museum for your geology edits; Robert McKenzie for helping me with my wonky pdf and cover concept. Angeliki Yannaghas at Stripy Duck Bookshop & Cafe, Bruton, for your encouragement and advice; Denise Outen & David Dawson for saying this idea has dino legs; Karen & Amber of Folde Dorset for cover ponderings and white space inspiration; Michael Fox for your precise advice; and to all the warm, inspiring people I met along this wondrous way.

Any mistakes?

Don't blame those above,

blame my *wonky* mind.

the sketches were spontaneously done in greyscale

Contact me or see more   iaindryden°com

Other works by Iain Dryden

Camino Voices - The voices of long distant walkers bring to life Northern Spain's 600 mile pilgrimage, illustrated with my sketches.

Tracing the Flow - Using doodling as a base, easy, proven exercises help relaxation and de-stressing.

Joyful Walking - Enhance your well-being by being attentive to the world, yourself and life, and simply through walking!

Other books in the above series are cooking.

Satya's Truths. (a novel) Ewan, an artist flees to India after an accidental crime. His constantly unpredictable adventure becomes an uncalled-for quest. The chaos, and three remarkable women, turn Ewan from a stiff upper-crust Englishman into a man capable of self understanding, empathy and even, he hopes, love.

Worldwide Copyright © - Iain Dryden 2024
registered March 2024 by iaindryden.com
Published by Crikey Books, Somerset.

crikey

books

Font - Avenir, generally size 9

A CIP catalogue record for this title is available from the British
Library.

ISBN -: 978-0-9934867-1-5

Printed & bound by Inky Little Fingers, Gloucester, GL2 8AX, UK

The paper used in this book comes from responsibly managed

and sustainable sources in Europe.

sustainably sourced paper

space for your own notes

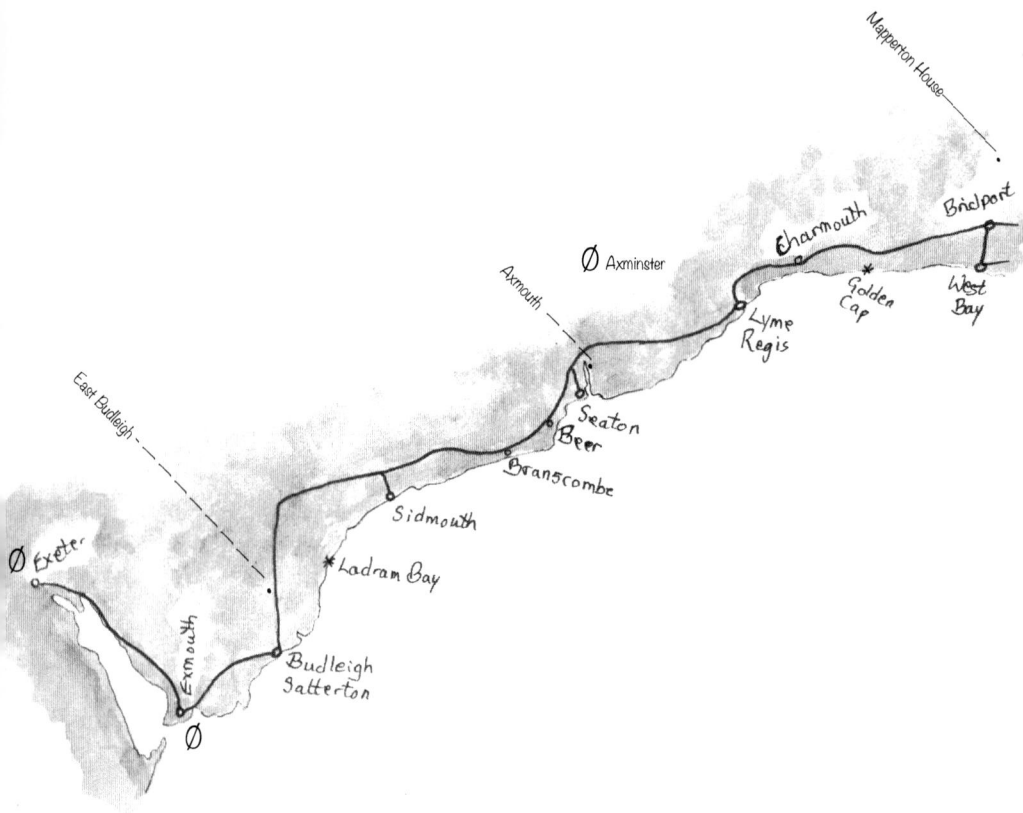

Mapperton House

Bridport

Charmouth
Golden
Cap
West
Bay

Ø Axminster

Axmouth

Lyme
Regis

East Budleigh

Seaton
Beer

Branscombe

Sidmouth

Ladram Bay

Ø Exeter

Exmouth

Budleigh
Salterton

Ø

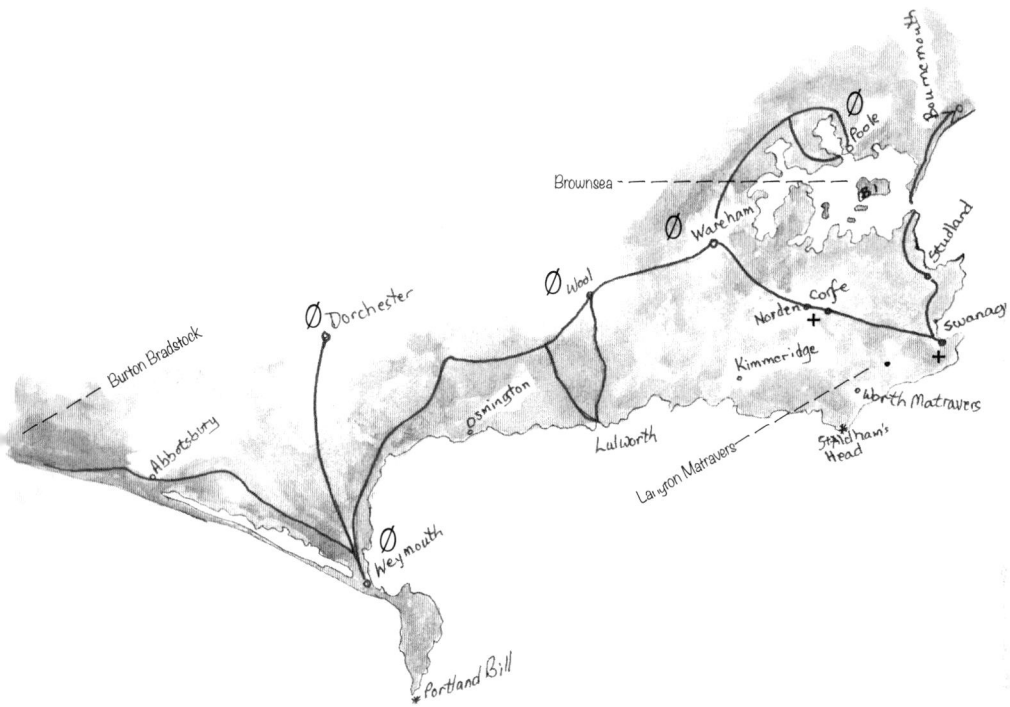

the jurassic coast

—— buses all year
Ø train stations
+ steam train

thank you